The Divine Feminine in Biblical Wisdom Literature

Books in the

SkyLight Illuminations Series

Bhagavad Gita: Annotated & Explained
The Book of Mormon: Selections Annotated & Explained
Dhammapada: Annotated & Explained
The Divine Feminine in Biblical Wisdom Literature: Selections Annotated & Explained
The Gospel of Philip: Annotated & Explained
The Gospel of Thomas: Annotated & Explained
Hasidic Tales: Annotated & Explained
The Hebrew Prophets: Selections Annotated & Explained
The Hidden Gospel of Matthew: Annotated & Explained
Native American Stories of the Sacred: Annotated & Explained
Rumi and Islam: Selections from His Stories, Poems, and Discourses—Annotated & Explained
The Secret Book of John: The Gnostic Gospel—Annotated & Explained
Selections from the Gospel of Sri Ramakrishna: Annotated & Explained
Spiritual Writings on Mary: Annotated & Explained
The Way of a Pilgrim: Annotated & Explained
Zohar: Annotated & Explained

The Divine Feminine in Biblical Wisdom Literature

Selections Annotated & Explained

Translation & Annotation
by Rabbi Rami Shapiro

Foreword by Rev. Cynthia Bourgeault, PhD

Walking Together, Finding the Way

SKYLIGHT PATHS®
PUBLISHING
Woodstock, Vermont

The Divine Feminine in Biblical Wisdom Literature: Selections Annotated & Explained

2005 First Printing

Library of Congress Cataloging-in-Publication Data
Shapiro, Rami M.
The divine feminine in biblical wisdom literature : selections annotated & explained : translation & annotation / Rami Shapiro ; foreword by Cynthia Bourgeault.
p. cm. — (SkyLight illuminations)
Includes bibliographical references (p.) and index.
ISBN 1-59473-109-8 (quality pbk. : alk. paper) 1. Wisdom (Biblical personification) 2. Bible. O.T.—Criticism, interpretation, etc. I. Bible. O.T. English. Shapiro. Selections. 2005. II. Title. III. Series.
BS580.W58S53 2005
223'.06—dc22 2005011663

10 9 8 7 6 5 4 3 2 1

Manufactured in the United States of America
Cover design: Walter C. Bumford III
Cover art: "Empyrean" by Marcia Snedecor, Ethereal Art, © 2005 by Marcia Snedecor

SkyLight Paths Publishing is creating a place where people of different spiritual traditions come together for challenge and inspiration, a place where we can help each other understand the mystery that lies at the heart of our existence.

SkyLight Paths sees both believers and seekers as a community that increasingly transcends traditional boundaries of religion and denomination—people wanting to learn from each other, *walking together, finding the way*.

Walking Together, Finding the Way
Published by SkyLight Paths Publishing
A Division of LongHill Partners, Inc.
Sunset Farm Offices, Route 4, P.O. Box 237
Woodstock, VT 05091
Tel: (802) 457-4000 Fax: (802) 457-4004
www.skylightpaths.com

Contents

What Does She Teach?

The Way of the Wise

Foreword

Rev. Cynthia Bourgeault, PhD

You are now holding in your hands a small treasure. Prepare to be delighted—and transformed.

When my friend Rami Shapiro asked me to contribute the foreword to his soon-to-be-published manuscript on the Divine Feminine in biblical Wisdom Literature, I agreed partly out of skepticism. The Divine Feminine in the Old Testament? It sounded like a major oxymoron. Back in seminary days, I'd been well steeped in the conventional understanding that the cornerstones of patriarchal consciousness in the West were laid down in the Hebrew Bible, making itself known through several spiritual non-negotiables: the utter transcendence of God, the unbridgeable abyss between Creator and created, the revulsion of anything remotely resembling "goddess worship." While I often privately suspected this was not the whole picture, as a Christian (and a woman), I didn't feel I had much of a platform on which to question another tradition's deepest self-understanding.

But when a *rabbi* tells me that this is not the whole picture, then I feel a tidal wave of validation, not only for his tradition but for my own as well. So it *is* true after all: there has been a feminine presence, a Wisdom presence, lurking all along at the root of our Jewish-Christian universe! Rami Shapiro not only makes a case for this, but spells it out chapter and verse by assembling the pertinent texts and allowing us to see for ourselves. He deftly sets the stage and lets Wisdom make Her own introductions.

Granted, Rami is not exactly your typical rabbi, and I suspect there are those among his colleagues who would be hard put to accord him the mantle of spokesperson for the tradition. I chuckled in bittersweet recognition when he shares his story of being upbraided at rabbinical school by a professor who informed him, "The only mother goddess we Jews have is Golda Meir." Among certain sectors of Judaism (and Christianity as well), the idea of a feminine presence in scripture will remain a hard sell. But Rami speaks from a deeper and more universal tradition, a Wisdom tradition, and within this more spacious context his beautiful words and teachings sparkle like clear water after a long drought.

I love where this book is coming from, but even more I love where it's headed. While acknowledging his early flirtations with a "Hebrew goddess," Rami does not remain at that level, but moves us swiftly to higher ground. Unlike so much naively reactionary feminism, he is very clear of the distinction between biological facts and theological archetypes, and does not try to make a case for Chochma, Wisdom, as a literal female consort of a male God. Rather, he sees in Wisdom a reflective principle, simultaneously creating and created in a seamless dance of divine becoming. Her proper role is not to be worshipped but to be actualized in the material of our own lives.

Rami clearly realizes that Chochma (or Sophia in Greek) is about Wisdom and that Wisdom is about transformation: "Not only an altered state of mind but an altered trait of behavior," as he so incisively observes. On the strength of this observation he is able to move us beyond the finger pointing to the moon (whether male or female) to the moon itself: the timeless universal teachings and practices that lead to a transformed heart and the permanent establishment within a person of *mochin d'gadlut*, or spacious mind. In his hands, the Wisdom teachings of the Hebrew Bible take their place within the deeper Wisdom of humanity, adding their individual voices to the universal message since time immemorial: Only through this transformation of the heart can humankind arrive at a stable and enduring peace.

I have long suspected that Jesus, too, emerges from such a greater Wisdom tradition, and Rami's work confirms and extends this insight in several fruitful—and potentially revolutionary—ways. His convincing case that *logos* ("the Word," which according to the Gospel of John, "became flesh and dwelled among us" in the person of Jesus) is in fact identical to Chochma/Sophia, Holy Wisdom, neatly removes an entire layer of theological superstructure that has been a barrier to understanding for both Christians and Jews. In this same stroke, it also situates Jesus firmly within the Wisdom tradition, as a *moshel moshelim* (a teacher of Wisdom) rather than the long-expected political messiah who for two thousand years has been the primary stumbling block to Jewish-Christian reconciliation. "Now a Wisdom Jesus I would have no problem with!" Rami shared with me in conversation. What seeds of healing—for both traditions—may lie hidden in this one seminal insight!

Finally, I love the way Rami gets there. This little book is vintage Rami Shapiro, masterfully conceived and elegantly executed. With clarity and concision he explains the tradition, assembles the pertinent texts, and presents them in crisp, clean translations with profound spiritual teaching and commentary discreetly disguised as notes. If you're like me, you'll find that this little volume very quickly makes itself indispensable. It's destined to become a spiritual classic, a core textbook in the library of worldwide Wisdom.

If the Mother has indeed been pursuing Rami Shapiro, as he intimates in his preface, She definitely picked the right man for the job. We are all the richer for their encounter.

Enjoy!

Preface

I first met Mother Wisdom, *Chochma* in Hebrew, *Sophia* in Greek, during my freshman year at the University of Massachusetts in Amherst. I had been studying the Hindu legends of Lord Shiva and His Consort Shakti and found striking parallels between them and their kabbalistic equivalents, *HaShem* (the Name, Y-H-V-H) and *Shekhinah* (the masculine and feminine aspects of God, respectively). I began to read all I could find on the Hebrew Goddess, as Raphael Patai called Her, and immersed myself in his work as well as the work of Erich Neumann, Robert Graves, and Johann Jakob Bachoven. During my junior year of college I presented a paper on the Hebrew Goddess to a select group of professors during a daylong conference convened to explore the Goddess in Hindu and kabbalistic thought.

I thought I was done with Her after that, yet several years later, when applying to rabbinical school at the Reconstructionist Rabbinical College, my work on the Mother was brought up to challenge the authenticity of my scholarship. While my study of the Hebrew Goddess was raw and certainly smacked of undergraduate overzealousness, and excess, it seemed to have offended several of the professors at RRC. "The only mother goddess we Jews have is Golda Meir," one professor said derisively. "Your work is bunk."

Needless to say, I didn't attend the Reconstructionist College and, when applying for admission to the Reform Movement's Hebrew Union College, I thought it best not to mention my affair with the Goddess. I had little contact with the Mother during my five years at Hebrew Union College. I imagine She was a bit miffed at me and kept Her distance. Indeed, it wasn't until the early 1990s that She came back into my life.

I was sitting at my kitchen table reading the *Miami Herald* and marveling at a wonderful oil painting of the Virgin Mary that was printed in full color above the fold on the front page. I could not take my eyes off it. The detail, the brushwork, the use of color—the whole thing captivated me; it looked like something van Gogh would have painted. I had yet to read the article, and just kept staring at the painting. Finally it dawned on me that I could see the painting in person if I read the text and found out which gallery was showing it.

As I read the accompanying article, I discovered that this was not a painting at all. It was an oil slick that appeared on the giant plate glass window of a bank in Clearwater, Florida. It was a miracle, a sign from the Virgin attesting to the truth of Her Son and Her compassion for humankind. Thousands of believers were streaming into Clearwater to see Her. I am not a believer and I didn't drive to the bank to pay homage. But if Muhammad won't come to the mountain …

After the incident at the bank, I began to see Her everywhere. And worse, She started talking to me. Knowing that owning up to Her cost me with the admissions committee of the Reconstructionist Rabbinical College, I'm not going to share the details of our conversations; suffice it to say that She intruded on my meditation and prayer time, and just would not leave me alone.

When I moved from Florida to Los Angeles and began running retreats out of La Casa de Maria, She had me. I would go for walks late at night and talk with Her. Just in case I was going to make the mistake of assuming She was Mary exclusively, She sent me up the road to the Vedanta Convent where I found Her in Hindu garb as the Mother, the Divine Feminine worshiped by Sri Ramakrishna.

I shared what was happening to me with my friend and teacher Andrew Harvey, a devotee of the Mother in all Her forms. "The Mother is chasing you," he said, "and you must surrender to Her." I protested his assessment and explained that I was having trouble reconciling Her with my personal nondualist and nongendered theology. "If God is everything," he said, "why can God not also be Mother? If God is everything, why can't God manifest as Other? She calls to everyone, and to ignore Her is to ignore the greatest gift you may ever be offered: the passionate embrace of the Mother. She is going to hound you until She has you, and then She is going to strip you of all your ideas and notions until there is nothing left to you but the ecstasy of Her embrace." I protested again, claiming that I couldn't embrace the Virgin; I am a Jew. With a look that said, "My poor, poor idiot friend," Andrew said to me, "It isn't Mary, but the Mother. She comes to the Christian as the Blessed Virgin; She comes to you as Chochma, Mother Wisdom." And with that my whole life changed.

Chochma, the Hebrew word for "wisdom," is the manifestation of the Divine Mother as She appears in the Hebrew Bible. She is the first manifestation of God, the vehicle of His unfolding, the Way of nature, the Way God is God in the world you and I experience every day. Seeing Her as Chochma removed the last of my defenses. I stopped running away, and gave myself to Her as best I could.

A few years later, I shared my experience of Mother Wisdom and Andrew's comments with another friend and teacher, Sister Mary Jose Hobday, a Native American medicine woman and Catholic nun. "You have to share this story with people," she told me. "It is what so many people are searching for. You have the credentials, the standing. If you say you know the Mother, talk with Her, and get guidance from Her, others will come forward and admit to the same."

"But this could ruin my career as a rabbi. Modern Jews can barely deal with God the Father, let alone God the Mother."

Sister Jose laughed at me. "Do you really think you have a choice in this?" As it turns out, I didn't. As I traveled the country running workshops and retreats, I found myself talking about Chochma more and more. She just insinuated Herself into the conversation. The first response from people was shock. Then, as I shared Her teachings found in sacred texts, both Hebrew and Greek, biblical and intertestamental, they began to relax, not because I had made Her kosher, but because what they heard in the text was what they somehow already knew in their hearts.

For the next few years I talked about Chochma but dared not write about Her. Then, over lunch with Jon Sweeney, former editor in chief at SkyLight Paths, I pitched the idea of a book for his SkyLight Illuminations series anthologizing and commenting on some of Her teachings. He jumped at the idea and this book was conceived.

What you hold in your hand is an invitation to find Chochma calling to you from every corner of your life. What I share with you here are some of the most powerful teachings found in the Jewish Wisdom Literature of the Hebrew and Greek Bibles. This material may be new to you, or it may be words you have read a hundred times. In either case I ask you to hear them as if for the first time; to hear them spoken by the Mother directly to you here and now. This is how they sound to me, and I will have failed both you and Her if I have not given them that immediacy in this collection.

This book is a selection of Her teachings only. Use it as a gateway to the rest. You will find in Her teachings an understanding of life and a way of living that can only deepen over time. "Her ways are ways of pleasantness, and all Her paths are peace" (Proverbs 3:17). May you be blessed to walk them with Her.

Acknowledgments

While all my writing is done alone, none is done in isolation. The quality of this book would not be what it is without the tireless efforts of my editor, Emily Wichland. I am as always grateful to her for playing midwife to my work. I am also grateful to all the wonderful people at SkyLight Paths with whom I have had the pleasure of working on three books over the years. Thank you all very much.

I also want to thank my wife, Debbie. If not for her unflagging support of me, my research, and my writing, I would have neither the time nor the freedom to do what I do. It is to her that this book is dedicated.

Introduction

I believe in revelation. I believe revelation comes to you when you slip from narrow mind, what the Jewish sages call *mochin d'katnut,* to spacious mind, *mochin d'gadlut*. Meditation, prayer, chanting, and study are four ways people have discovered for shifting from narrow mind to spacious mind. I believe that both minds are involved in the process of revelation: *Mochin d'gadlut* receives it and *mochin d'katnut* applies it. In this way revelation is not only an altered state of mind (moving from narrow to spacious), but an altered trait of behavior, moving from selfishness, fear, and narcissism to justice, compassion, and humility. There is nothing mysterious about revelation. It is not concerned with esoteric doctrines or beliefs. You do not believe in revelation because it is absurd (*Credo quia absurdum*, Tertullian), but because it is direct, personal, rational, and intrinsically compelling. It honors both self and other. You know it is revelation because you know it is true, and not the other way around.

I do not believe that revelation and scripture are interchangeable. I do not believe that everything that passes for holy writ is from God. On the contrary, I believe that much of what is called holy is simply the opinions of those who profit from others believing it is holy. I find it difficult to believe that the details of priestly dress and function found in Torah come from God. It seems much more logical to believe that they come from the Levites themselves as they are the only ones who benefit from the pomp and power that go with the priestly cult.

Similarly, I cannot reconcile the God who says "Love your neighbor as yourself" (Leviticus 19:18) with the God who says it is permissible to kill a person who picks up sticks on a Saturday (Numbers 15:35). I find it much more logical to believe that the first comes from *mochin d'gadlut* while the second comes from *mochin d'katnut*. I think you can actually go through the sacred texts of every religion and make similar distinctions. And when you do you will find a great similarity between the two types of material regardless of which scripture it comes from.

The texts that come from narrow mind (as opposed to those that come from spacious mind and are filtered through narrow mind) are fear-based, and serve to enforce the power of the few over the many. The teachings that come from spacious mind are rooted in love and compassion, and serve to establish justice irrespective of rank.

The texts in this book are revelation. They come from God through the spacious mind of the teachers of Wisdom. They do not speak of power or rank; they do not elevate one group over another, even though they clearly prefer the wise to the foolish. They are not limited to the Chosen or the Saved. They are spoken to the world through a people, but not to that people alone. They are simple, direct, and compelling. They are to be lived and not simply learned. And they are rarely taught.

Why? First because Wisdom is a woman and women haven't fared well in the Western religious tradition of the past three thousand years. While you can point out significant exceptions, the norm in Judaism, Christianity, and Islam is to downplay the role of women. One way to do that is to ignore the role of the Mother, Chochma, in creation and the life of us creatures.

It is no small thing to note that Wisdom is feminine. The original language of the texts, both Hebrew and Greek, make this very clear: Hebrew *Chochma* and Greek *Sophia* are both feminine nouns. The authors of the Wisdom books took this gender specificity seriously and envisioned Wisdom as Mother, God's consort and bride, the Divine Feminine through which the masculine God fashioned all creation. Further, they saw in the union of masculine and feminine a powerful analogy for the greater unity of all in the ineffable Godhead that transcends our imagination.

To keep the power of their language before us I refer to Wisdom as She and to God as He, knowing that it is in the unity of the two that the full Godhead is manifest. It is important that you do not mistake my use of language for something it is not. I do not believe that God is literally male or that Chochma is literally female. We are not dealing with biological facts but with theological archetypes residing within each of us. What is needed is a marriage of the two within the individual.

The unity of these forces creates a new person, the divine *anthropos*, the fully integrated human who is called the sage in these Wisdom books. The sage, regardless of gender, is married to Chochma; he or she is the partner of the Divine Feminine.

You and I have the capacity to be sages. As you read the teachings of Mother Wisdom, know that She is speaking to you, inviting you to Her home, to Her hearth, to Her teachings that you may become a sage. As the Divine Feminine, Wisdom can appear to you as Mother, Lover, Bride, Sister, or any number of feminine archetypal forms. For me she is Mother above all, and it is as Mother that I most often address Her. Find the image that best suits you, and allow it to open you to the way that leads to the birth of the divine *anthropos* within you.

Another reason for ignoring the teachings of Chochma is that She is intrinsically antiestablishment and nonhierarchical. Wisdom is taught, so the student needs a teacher, but once She is learned there is a great leveling: Teacher and student share the same understanding. "Behold, days are coming ... when I will seal a new covenant with the House of Israel and with the House of Judah.... I will place My Teaching within them and I will write it on their heart.... They will no longer teach one another, saying, Know the Lord! for everyone will know Me, from the smallest to the greatest" (Jeremiah 31:30–33).

At the heart of corporate religion is the question of power: Who rules over whom? From the priestly tribe of Levites to the priestly class of the Church to the learned rabbis and imams, there is in corporate religious life a hierarchy of power supporting a ruling elite that claims to have a more direct connection to God than the rest of us. Chochma and Her teachings are a direct challenge to this hierarchy. For Wisdom there are only two kinds of people—the wise and foolish. The wise listen to Her, the foolish ignore Her, but She is available to both at any time. The fool who seeks Wisdom is welcome, and in time will become wise. Her desire parallels that of God's in Exodus 19:6: "You shall be a nation of priests." A nation of priests is a nation without a priesthood, without a religious elite. The people soon abandon God's dream and establish not only a priestly tribe, the Levites, but also a hierarchy within the priesthood, the *Kohanim*, led by Moses' brother Aaron and Aaron's sons and male descendents.

Chochma doesn't forget Her dream. She gives Herself freely to all. You may choose to reject Her, but She will not reject you. Chochma stands on the street corners and calls to you, "Pay heed to me, for happy are those who keep to My paths. Listen to My instruction and become wise, and do not turn away.… Find Me and find life! Hate Me and love death" (Proverbs 8:32–36). It is not Chochma who hates you, but you who hate Her. Her love is constant, though She will not spare you the consequences of your foolishness.

The third reason She is known so rarely, then, is that those who could point Her out to us have no incentive for doing so. A priest or minister who can convince you that priestcraft is essential to your salvation has just secured a job for life. Rabbis or imams who can convince you that the proper (i.e., their) understanding of revelation and law are essential to your salvation have done the same. But what do these leaders get from introducing you to Mother Wisdom? A pink slip. You don't need an intermediary when dealing with Wisdom. Yes, there are sages who can bring you closer to Her, but once your yearning for Her has been kindled by the sage, She is willing to teach you Herself, and in so doing erases any permanent hierarchy of power. You begin at the feet of a sage, but in the end you stand alone with Her.

Chochma doesn't serve anyone's quest for power and control over others. Her gift is power and control over yourself. That is why She is so rarely taught, and that is why She is so desperately needed.

Having made a case for studying Wisdom, let's get a sense of just who She is.

> The Lord created Me at the beginning of His work, the first of His ancient acts.
> I was established ages ago, at the beginning of the beginning, before the earth …
> When He established the heavens, I was already there.
> When He drew a circle on the face of the deep,
> When He made firm the skies above,
> When he established the fountains feeding the seas below …
> I was beside Him, the master builder.
> I was His daily delight, rejoicing before Him always,
> Rejoicing in His inhabited world, and delighting in the human race.
>
> —Proverbs 8:22–31

Chochma was not simply the first of God's creations; She was the means through which all the others came forth. This is what it means to be the *master builder.* Chochma is both created and creative. She is the ordering principle of creation: "She embraces one end of the earth to the other, and She orders all things well" (Wisdom of Solomon 8:1). To know Her is to know the Way of all things, and thus to be able to act in harmony with them. To know the Way of all things and to act in accord with it is what it means to be wise.

To know Wisdom is to become wise. To become wise is to find happiness and peace: "Her Ways are ways of pleasantness, and all Her Paths are peace. She is a Tree of Life to those who lay hold of Her; those who hold Her close are happy" (Proverbs 3:17–18). Wisdom is not to be taken on faith. She is testable. If you follow Her you will find joy, peace, and happiness not at the end of the journey but as the very stuff of which the journey is made. This is crucial: The reward for following Wisdom is immediate. The Way to is the Way of.

Even one with only a slight knowledge of the Bible may note the radical departure from orthodoxy here. The Book of Genesis makes it very clear that God expels the first earthlings from the Garden of Eden lest they grasp hold of and take from the Tree of Life at the center of the Garden (Genesis 3:24). Yet here we are told that Wisdom Herself is the Tree of Life and that the whole point of life is to grab hold of Her and become one with Her. Why the difference?

This bit of Genesis speaks from a place of fear, the place of *mochin d'katnut,* narrow mind. Proverbs, in this case, speaks from the place of love, the place of *mochin d'gadlut,* spacious mind. Narrow mind is afraid of what will happen if you grasp hold of the Tree of Life. Not that you will live forever, stuck in an endless time line of moment after moment, but that you will slip out of time into eternity, out of self into Self, out of narrowness into spaciousness. This is the promise of Mother Wisdom—pleasantness and peace in the eternal now.

The key to the awakening that is Wisdom is having a clear perception of reality. Wisdom does not lead you to this clarity; She is this clarity. Imagine that you wake up in the middle of the night to find a snake coiled at the end of your bed. You freeze in fear, and spend the rest of the night awake, afraid, and unable to move. As dawn bathes your bedroom in soft light, you suddenly realize that the "snake" is simply the belt that you forgot to put away as you undressed the night before. The fear ends as quickly as it arose. Nothing has changed but the quality of your perception. You see clearly and can respond to what is rather than to what you imagined.

This is how Mother Wisdom works. She doesn't change anything; She illumines everything. She is right seeing. Chochma "pervades and penetrates" all things (Wisdom of Solomon 7:24). She is the ordering principle of the universe. What you see when you see Her is analogous to seeing the grain in wood, the current of wind and oceans, and the laws of nature, both the macrocosmic and the microcosmic. Just as you cannot separate the grain from the wood, or the current from the wind, or law from nature, you cannot separate Wisdom from creation. She is the Way things are.

You do not pray to Her or choose Her; you simply see Her and work in harmony with Her. Wisdom operates for you whether or not you appreciate Her. What distinguishes the wise from the foolish is their ability to distinguish between a belt and a snake.

How do you become wise? "The beginning of Wisdom is this: Get Wisdom!" (Proverbs 4:7). While this teaching may seem solipsistic, it actually reveals an important aspect of Chochma: The way to Wisdom is Wisdom Herself. You do not work your way toward Her; you take hold of Her from the beginning. As your relationship deepens, your clarity of seeing improves, but from the beginning you have Her and She has you: "I am my Beloved's and my Beloved is mine" (Song of Songs 2:16).

The Way of Wisdom is study, observation, and clear perception. What you study, observe, and perceive is Wisdom as well, for She is both the Way to and the Way of. Wisdom "knows and understands all things" (Wisdom of Solomon 9:10) because She is the creative energy through which God fashions all things. To know Her is to know the Way of all things. But you cannot study Chochma in the abstract, for there is no abstract with Her. You study Chochma by studying life and the myriad living beings that comprise life.

Chochma is not a reluctant guide or a hidden guru. She is not hard to find, nor does She require any austere test to prove you are worthy of Her. Rather She "stands on the hilltops, on the sidewalks, at the crossroads, at the gateways" (Proverbs 8:1–11) and calls to you to follow Her. Wisdom's only desire is to teach you to become wise. Her only frustration is your refusal to listen to Her.

The Bible is not reticent to sing Chochma's praises. She is "intelligent, holy, unique, subtle, flowing, transparent, and pure; She is distinct, invulnerable, good, keen, irresistible, and gracious; She is humane, faithful, sure, calm, all-powerful, all-seeing, and available to all who are intelligent, pure, and altogether simple" (Wisdom of Solomon 7:22–23). Clearly Chochma rivals God in many ways, but this is not surprising, for She is the Way God is manifest in the world. To know Her is to know God as well.

> Search for Her and seek Her out, and She will reveal Herself to you. When you lay hold of Her, do not let Her go. Take your rest with Her at last, and She will become ecstasy for you.
>
> —Wisdom of Jesus ben Sirach, 6:27–28

If Wisdom is both the teacher and the taught, then following Her is becoming intimate with Her. The Hebrew verb "to know" means both intellectual knowing and sexual intimacy. To know Wisdom is to be Her lover, and by loving Her you become God's beloved as well, for "the Lord loves those who love Her" (Wisdom of Jesus ben Sirach 4:14).

How are you to love Chochma? By knowing Her. Since She isn't separate from creation, your love of Her is a love of nature. You know Her by knowing how She manifests in the world as the world. You know Her, the Way of life, when you know the ways of the living.

The Way of Wisdom is not the "way of why" but the "way of what." The Hebrew word *chochma* can be read as *choach mah,* "what is." Wisdom will not tell you why things are the way they are, but will show you what they are and how you can live in harmony with them. Living in harmony with what is does not mean that you are passive and incapable of effecting change. It means that you will move the world the way a ship captain moves a large ship.

You turn a boat by turning its rudder. On large vessels, however, the weight of the water pressing against the massive rudder makes the direct turning of the rudder impossible. Instead, you turn a trimtab, a small rudder that allows you to turn the larger rudder, which ultimately turns the ship. Working with Wisdom you learn how to trimtab, to make small, subtle changes that effect larger ones. You learn how to cut with the grain, tack with the wind, swim with the current, and allow the nature of things to support your efforts. She will not tell you why things are the way they are, but She will make plain to you what things are and how you can deal with them to your mutual benefit.

It is my hope that this small selection of Wisdom's teachings will act like a trimtab in your life, moving you to open to Her, and find, in Her ways, of pleasantness and peace.

About the Wisdom Literature

Wisdom Literature comprises the Hebrew books Psalms (Heb., *Tehillim*), Proverbs (Heb., *Mishle*), Job (Heb., *Iyov*), *Song of Songs* (Heb., *Shir haShirim*), and Ecclesiastes (Heb., *Kohelet*), plus the Greek texts *Wisdom of Solomon* and *Wisdom of Jesus ben Sirach*. Each of these books is of Jewish origin, and all but *Wisdom of Solomon* and *Sirach* are found in the third section of the Hebrew *TaNaKH* (an acronym for *Torah*, the Five Books of Moses; *Nevi'im*, the Prophets; and *Ketuvim*, the Writings), or what is often called the Original, First, or Old Testament. The other two books are found in the *Apocrypha*, Jewish writings from the intertestamental period that are part of the Catholic Canon but not the Jewish or Protestant ones.

The Book of *Tehillim*/Psalms

Only a few of the 150 Psalms of the Hebrew Bible are considered part of the Wisdom Literature. Scholars cannot agree as to what exactly constitutes a Wisdom Psalm. They do not share a distinctive literary style, and the criteria used to define them rely on philosophical content they share with other Wisdom Books. Because scholars have not reached a consensus on how many "wisdom traits" a psalm must have in order to qualify as a Wisdom Psalm, it is difficult to speak authoritatively about this small body of work. Most scholars agree, however, that Psalms 1, 34, 37, 49, 111, and 112 are Wisdom Psalms. These Psalms are less praises of God than instructions to those who would be sages.

> Happy is one who walks not in the counsel of the wicked, and stands not in the path of the sinful, and sits not in the gatherings of cynics, but whose desire is for the Torah of God and in God's Torah he meditates day and night.
>
> —Psalm 1:1–2

> Do you desire life, and long days for seeing goodness? Then guard your tongue from evil, and your lips from speaking lies. Turn from evil and do good; seek peace and pursue it.
>
> —Psalm 34:13–15

> Wait in silence for *HaShem* ... desist from anger and abandon wrath ... the meek shall inherit the earth.... The mouth of the righteous utters wisdom, their tongues speak justly, the Torah of God is in their hearts.
>
> —Psalm 37:7, 8, 11, 30

> My mouth will speak wisdom, and the meditations of my heart are insightful. I will incline my ear to the parable; with a harp I will solve my riddle.
>
> —Psalm 49:4–6

> The beginning of Wisdom is the awe of *HaShem*, good understanding to all those who practice Wisdom.
>
> —Psalm 111:10

> [The sage] is gracious, compassionate, and righteous. Good is one who graciously lends; who conducts all affairs with justice.
>
> —Psalm 112:4–5

The Book of *Mishle*/Proverbs

The Book of Proverbs comprises thirty-one chapters and 915 verses, each attributed to King Solomon. There is no evidence to back up this claim, however, and the claim itself rests solely on the reputation of Solomon as the wisest person of his day.

> God gave Solomon wisdom, discernment, and understanding as vast as the sands on the seashore. His wisdom surpassed the wisdom of all the peoples East, and all the wisdom of Egypt. He was wiser than anyone ... [and] his fame spread throughout all the surrounding nations. He composed three thousand proverbs, and his songs num-

> bered a thousand and five.... People from all nations came to hear the wisdom of Solomon.
>
> —1 Kings 4:29–34, Revised Standard Version

The Talmud claims that Solomon wrote the Song of Songs in his youth, Proverbs in middle age, and Ecclesiastes in old age, and dates the editing of the Book of Proverbs to the eighth century BCE during the reign of King Hezekiah (*Bava Batra* 15a). While most scholars agree that the Book of Proverbs is an anthology of teachings spanning several centuries, there is no reason to doubt that some of the material dates from Solomon's time and was written by the king himself.

The Book of Proverbs contains many literary forms, but the dominant one is parallelism. The Proverbs are often presented as couplets with the second verse either a rejection of or an affirmation of the first verse. For example:

> Does not Wisdom call,
> and does not Understanding raise Her voice? (8:1)
>
> Take My instruction instead of silver,
> And knowledge rather than fine gold. (8:10)

The Hebrew for "proverb," *mashal*, is a difficult word to define. The three-letter Hebrew root *m-sh-l* can be read as a noun, proverb or parable, or as a verb—"to compare," "to be like," and "to rule or govern." The first points to the power of analogy, which dominates the Book of Proverbs, the second to the fact that these analogies are thought to reveal patterns of truth that govern nature, human and otherwise. The truth of a proverb is self-evident. You only have to hear a proverb once and you will know it is true. It is as if the proverb reflected truths already embedded in the human psyche as well as in the doings of the nonhuman world of nature.

One aspect of life that is missing in the Proverbs is death. Without any belief in an afterlife, the authors of Proverbs found death simply part of life, and saw no reason to lament it or defeat it. Wisdom is essential to living life well, but even She cannot prevent you from dying. Birth and death are not problems to these sages. What matters is how you spend the days in between.

There are two types of people according to Proverbs: those who are wise and those who are foolish. The wise spend their days in harmony with Chochma, aligning themselves with the natural order of things. In so doing they become simple, marveling at the innate complexity of life without adding unnecessary complications to it. These wise and simple people are the sages. The foolish follow their own designs and run headlong into immutable Wisdom. The wise are thought to be good and honorable for they uphold the Way of life. The foolish are not simply foolish but wicked, for they seek to overturn the Way of life and replace the order established by God with the disorder that comes from human greed.

While there is but one category of sage, fools come in eight varieties:

1. *pethi*, ignorant
2. *k'sil*, dimwitted
3. *'wil*, obstinate
4. *sakal*, addicts
5. *ba'ar*, boors
6. *nabal*, brutes
7. *holel*, insane
8. *lesh*, narcissistic

Of these eight, only the first was teachable; the rest, the authors of Proverbs thought, were beyond hope.

The wise differ from the foolish in several characteristics. The wise control their tongue, honor silence, and know how to use words to help people align with Wisdom. They control their passions, and engage life with purpose. The foolish, on the other hand, are victims of their emotions, buffeted about by circumstance. What marks a fool most of all is sexual license, drunkenness, sloth, and gossip.

A whore is a like a bottomless pit,
Sexual adventures like a well too narrow for a bucket.
Desire lies in wait like a thief,
And robs you of what little faith you may have.

—Proverbs 23:27–28

Who suffers? Who moans? Who struggles needlessly? Who complains endlessly?

Those who linger long over wine …

—Proverbs 23:29ff

Too much sleep, too much slumber, a compulsion to nap,
And poverty will sneak up behind you like a bum, and desire like an armed robber.

—Proverbs 6:10–11

Too much talk leads to error,
the wise restrain their lips.

—Proverbs 10:19

Wild sex, drunkenness, laziness, and gossip are the opposite of the Way, and allegiance to them makes you an enemy of the Way and the One who founded it. To resist the allure of these negative forces, the sages suggest you immerse yourself in Wisdom.

The Book of *Iyov*/Job

The Book of Job is a brilliant piece of philosophical literature, blending both poetry and prose in forty-two chapters and 1,070 verses. The text can be divided into two sections, defined by their linguistic styles. The older and shorter section is prose, and is used to introduce and conclude the longer poetic section, which works out the philosophical problems raised by Job and his friends. The prose piece most likely comes from an earlier pre-Hebraic tale that the author of Job then adapted to suit a desire to reflect on the nature of suffering.

The plot has to do with a righteous man named Job whom God gives over to Satan. Satan is certain that under the proper circumstances Job will lose his faith in God and, in the words of Job's wife, "curse God and die like a man" (Job 2:9). God, on the other hand, trusts that Job will find a way to handle suffering that does not cause him to lose faith.

Satan kills Job's children, bankrupts his business, and infects his body with boils, leaving Job to sit in the ruins of his once-magnificent life using the sharp edges of broken pottery jars to scratch the incessant itching of his oozing sores.

Hearing of his fate, Job's friends—Elophaz the Temanite, Dildad the Shuhite, Zophar the Naamathite, and Elihu son of Barachel the Buzite—travel to Job's side to comfort him. Certain that a loving and just God would not allow such a horror to befall a righteous man, they are convinced that Job himself brought on his own misfortune. His righteousness is a sham, and he must admit his sins and throw himself on the mercy of the Merciful God. Job, on the other hand, will admit no such thing, and insists that God Himself come and explain the reason for his suffering.

Thus far the Book of Job is a skillful exploration of the reasons for suffering, but the book becomes something more when God appears to Job and the two engage in conversation, albeit a lopsided one. Speaking from a whirlwind, God scoffs at the arguments of Job's friends. Rather than offering a true understanding of suffering and explaining why it is that the good Job suffers so, God seems to ignore the issue of suffering altogether and begins to pepper Job with a series of questions designed to overwhelm and silence him.

The Book of Job never answers the question of why Job suffers, and yet God's revelation to Job does seem to provide him with a sense of peace. After accepting God's teaching, Job is returned to health, wealth, and given new children. But just what did Job learn?

Job asks God to explain the reason for suffering. Does God do that? Or does God ignore Job's plea and simply seek to humble him before the grandeur of God? Or does God use the awesomeness of His power to instill in Job a sense of trust, saying in effect, "You cannot understand the nature of Nature, so how are you going to understand the nature of suffering. Trust Me, I know what I am doing."

Given the endless speculation regarding God's response to Job, the subject of the book is also open to question. Is Job exploring the reality of innocent suffering? Is the book promoting surrender and blind trust in God? Is it suggesting that the best way to deal with suffering is to cultivate detachment rooted in faith? Or is the book an attack on the very notion of a just God, positing instead an all-powerful despot who need not render accounts to anyone?

It is the open-ended nature of the Book of Job that keeps it alive in the minds of readers and commentators. Most religious commentators take the Book of Job to be an affirmation that there are things that human beings cannot know, and that accepting the unknowability of things is the key to faith. Commentators often speak of the "patience of Job" referring to his supposed willingness to endure whatever suffering befell him without loss of faith. In fact, however, Job is not patient at all. His faith demands answers, and he insists that God explain Himself.

It is this insistence that leads to the core challenge of the Book of Job. While on the surface the book seems to deal with the nature of suffering, the real issue is the nature of God. Is God just or not? Is God's world ruled by order or by chaos?

At the heart of the Wisdom Tradition is the notion that the universe is governed by order. The Book of Job challenges not the order of the universe but the tendency among humans to equate order with justice. Justice here is thought of in terms of quid pro quo; you reap what you sow. But Job sowed only righteousness and reaped only suffering. Where is the justice in that?

God's response to Job is to shift the discussion from justice to order. God points out to Job that rain falls "on land where no one lives, on desert sands, devoid of human life," on land that cannot possibly benefit from it (Job 38:26–27). Rain in the Hebrew Bible is associated with reward: "If you continually hearken to My commandments ... then I will provide rain for your land in the proper season" (Deuteronomy 11:13–14). The Book of Job is a radical departure from the Five Books of Moses, severing the link between nature and justice. Nature has an order, but it is not necessarily a moral one. Morality cannot be linked to the contingencies of mortal life such as sickness, accident, old age, and death. All beings suffer, all beings die, regardless of their ethics and just deeds.

This revelation may well be a surprise to Job, but not to the reader. The prose prologue tells us that Job is a righteous man without blemish, and thus all the suffering he endures has nothing to do with his guilt or innocence. It is not a punishment for injustice but a test of his faith. The question is, faith in what?

The real point of the Book of Job may have less to do with what God says to Job than with the fact that God chooses to show up at all. It is in the midst of life's most wrenching moments that the person of faith encounters God. And that encounter always places suffering in a larger context. What God seems to say to Job is this: There is a deep order to the world, despite all the chaos you see. As long as you seek to make sense out of the chaos, you will fail. But if you can broaden your perspective and see the whole rather than your particular part, you will find that your life is simply one part of a greater drama, the meaning of which you cannot fathom.

The silence of Job before God's revelation is not the silence of a man diminished, but the silence of a sage awakened. Job falls silent because words are useless at this point. There is nothing he or God can say that can capture the enormity of Reality. Only when words cease can the Truth be found. Job ends his encounter with God this way: "In the past I had heard You with my ears; now I see You with my eyes. Therefore, I surrender to the silence, knowing I am dust and ash" (Job 42:5–6).

In other words, Job says that his knowledge of God and God's plan was a matter of hearsay, secondhand talk that could not even approximate the Truth. Now he sees the truth for himself, and it renders him empty, humble, and silent. Words cannot convey what Job now knows. His silence is more profound than speech; his faith is now rooted in reality rather than abstractions.

The Song of Songs

The Song of Songs (Heb., *Shir haShirim*) is one of the most controversial books in the Hebrew Bible. The opening verse, "The Song of Songs by Solomon," seems to ascribe the song to King Solomon. The Hebrew is less clear, because the preposition *l'* in *l'Shlomo* could be read "by Solomon," "for Solomon," and even "concerning Solomon." Traditionally, however, the book is credited to Solomon.

While the authorship of the book is open to debate, the importance of the song itself is not. When the late-first-century Rabbis in Yavneh were deciding the final version of the Hebrew Canon, the debate over the Song of Songs had to do with whether it should be retained as part of the canon, and not whether it should be added to the canon. The Song had long been a part of the sacred literature of the Jewish people.

The problem with the text was its overt sexuality. Because Solomon was considered the author, and because the Rabbis were able to read the song allegorically as a love story between God and Israel rather than between a human man and woman, they enshrined this book in the canon.

Solomon's status as the wisest of the wise was uncontested: "Solomon's wisdom surpassed the wisdom of all the peoples of the East, and all the wisdom of Egypt.... He composed three thousand proverbs, and his songs numbered one thousand and five" (1 Kings 4:29–34, Revised Standard Version). One of those proverbs states, "There are three things too wonderful for me, four that surpass my understanding: the way of an eagle in the sky, the way of a serpent upon a rock, the way of a ship in the midst of the sea, and the way of a man with a woman" (Proverbs 30:18–19). We could read the Song of Songs as Solomon's detailed exploration of this proverbial mystery.

Another aspect of the Song that spoke in its favor was its literary style. If Solomon were the greatest sage and he composed songs, songwriting itself was a skill of the wise.

Modern scholars, however, discount the idea of Solomon as the author of the Song, some even suggesting that the author was most likely a woman. Given the fact that 61.5 of the Song's 117 verses are written in a woman's voice, that women predominate in the book, that the song is free from any sexual discrimination against women, and that mothers are mentioned but not fathers, there is reason to believe that the Song of Songs was part of a song cycle written by the ancient Israelite women (see Judges 5; 1 Samuel 18:6–7; 2 Samuel 1:20, 24; Jeremiah 9:17, 20; and Ezekiel 32:16).

The Hebrew text of the Song available to us today is most likely almost identical to the original. Four ancient manuscripts of the Song of Songs have been found at Qumran, dating from sometime between 30 BCE and 70 CE, and all four support what is considered the canonical Hebrew text. Dating the text itself, however, is nearly impossible.

The Song of Songs is a love ballad between a man and a woman written largely from the woman's perspective. Within the context of Wisdom Literature, the Song is read as a love story between Chochma (the woman in the Song) and the sage (the man). Since Chochma calls to both men and women, we can read the Song more broadly, stepping outside the sexual politics of ancient Israel and realizing that the love of any sage, male or female, for Mother Wisdom is as passionate as the Song's evocation.

Kohelet/Ecclesiastes

No less than the Book of Job, Ecclesiastes is a blatant attack on the normative philosophy of its day, and one that is no less challenging in our own.

Ecclesiastes is the Greek translation of the original Hebrew title *Kohelet*. Both words mean "assembler" and refer to the fact that the book is a compilation of Wisdom Teachings ascribed to King Solomon. The book is a series of sermons on various topics spanning twelve chapters. The literary form of Ecclesiastes, called the Royal Testament, is rarely found among the books of the Hebrew Bible, though it was common in ancient Egypt. A Royal Testament is a first-person monologue whose sole authority comes from the life experience of the author. The Royal Testament style attests to one of the key aspects of Wisdom: She is revealed by human observation rather than divine revelation.

The observing human in this case is King Solomon: "I, Kohelet, was king over Israel in Jerusalem" (Ecclesiastes 1:12), and the book opens with "The words of Kohelet, son of David, king in Jerusalem" (Ecclesiastes 1:1). According to some Rabbis (*Bava Batra* 14a), King Hezekiah wrote the book with the help of his literati. Scholars date the book to the late third century BCE.

Perhaps the most famous line of Ecclesiastes is the second, *hevel havalim*. Usually translated as "Vanity of vanities, says Kohelet, vanity of vanities! All is vanity!" (Ecclesiastes 1:2), a more accurate rendering is this: "Emptiness upon emptiness, says Kohelet, emptiness upon emptiness! Everything is as transient as breath." The Hebrew word *hevel* means "breath" or "vapor" (see Isaiah 57:13 and Psalm 62:9), and implies that life is impermanent and transient rather than vain or meaningless. Throughout the Books of Psalms and Job, *hevel* is the term used to explain human life: We are mortal; there is nothing lasting in us.

Kohelet's concern is not that life is worthless, but that living a life based on the hope of permanence is foolish and actually prevents you from living well.

"What do people gain from all their toil under the sun?" (Ecclesiastes 1:3). Nothing. There is nothing to gain, for gain implies permanence. All the time you spend stockpiling things for the future is simply robbing yourself of enjoying the present. "There is nothing better for mortals than to eat and drink, and find enjoyment in their toil. This also, I saw, is from the hand of God" (Ecclesiastes 2:24).

The impermanence of life, Kohelet's first teaching, does not preclude there being an order to life, Kohelet's second teaching, and he takes pains to reveal that order. "The sun rises, sets, and rises again. The wind blows south and then north, round and round the wind blows following its circuit" (Ecclesiastes 1:5–6). Kohelet also makes it clear that human beings cannot affect that order: The laws of nature are not linked to human behavior and have nothing to do with reward or punishment. "What is crooked cannot be made straight; and what is absent cannot be counted" (Ecclesiastes 1:15).

What we can and must do is come to understand the order and seek to work in concert with it. "For everything there is a season, and a time for every purpose under heaven: moments for birth, and moments for death; moments for planting and moments for reaping; moments for killing and moments for healing; moments for destroying and moments for creating; moments for crying and moments for laughing; moments for mourning and moments for dancing" (Ecclesiastes 3:1–4).

Knowing what time it is reveals what needs to be done at that moment. The challenge is that the times cannot be predicted. This is Kohelet's third teaching: the unknowability of life. You cannot know when to mourn until it is time to mourn. In other words, the act and the time are the same.

Since you cannot know in advance what behavior is appropriate, to understand Wisdom as the accumulation of knowledge is to misunderstand Her entirely. Kohelet is saying that Wisdom is not something you can gain, but rather a way of living in which you must engage. Indeed the key to Wisdom is Her unknowability. You cannot know in the abstract. All you can do is engage life in the here and now, and act in accord with conditions as they arise. The meaning of life is in living: "*na'aseh v'nishmah*, we will do, and through our doing we will understand" (Exodus 24:7).

Wisdom of Solomon

The only Wisdom text to be originally composed in Greek, the Wisdom of Solomon was written to uplift the spirits of those Jews living in exile during the Greco-Roman era, and acted as a polemic against those gentiles who derided Judaism. While ascribing its authorship to King Solomon, the Wisdom of Solomon is the work of an unknown Jewish sage writing in Alexandria, Egypt, sometime during the last centuries BCE and first centuries CE.

For the author of the Wisdom of Solomon, Wisdom is the embodiment of God's will, and the agent for rewarding the righteous and punishing the wicked. Those whom Wisdom saves will live forever, while those She condemns will suffer in the afterlife, a concept not found in other Wisdom Books. The Wisdom of Solomon goes far beyond any of the other Wisdom books in linking Wisdom with God.

Wisdom is "a breath of the power of God, and pure emanation of God's Glory" (Wisdom of Solomon 7:25). Wisdom is the image of God's goodness (7:26) and the embodiment of the divine attributes: intelligent, holy, unique, subtle, flowing, transparent, pure, distinct, invulnerable, good, keen, irresistible, gracious, humane, faithful, sure, calm, all-powerful, all-seeing, and available to all who are intelligent, pure, and altogether simple (Wisdom of Solomon 7:22–23).

The author of the Wisdom of Solomon goes beyond even this description and tells readers that Wisdom "reaches mightily from one end of the earth to the other, and She orders all things well" (Wisdom of Solomon 8:1). In this, Wisdom and God are all but indistinguishable.

This makes the relationship between Wisdom and King Solomon all the more intriguing. According to the Wisdom of Solomon, Chochma and God are partners and Chochma and Solomon are partners. In a sense, the Divine Feminine is married not only to God but to all who are wise. The implication is that those created in the image and likeness of God (Genesis 1:26) can do as God does, and find union with and delight in the love of Wisdom.

The Wisdom of Jesus Ben Sirach

The full name of the author of this text is Shimon ben Yeshua ben Eleazar ben Sira, and he wrote this book in Hebrew sometime before 180 BCE.

Ben Sirach's grandson translated the book into Greek sometime after 132 BCE. The Hebrew version did not survive intact, though the text was preserved in Greek, Latin, and Syriac. Since the early 1900s, however, fragments of the Hebrew text have surfaced in Qumran, Masada, and the Genizah (storage room) of a medieval Cairo synagogue, and today two-thirds of the original Hebrew has been recovered.

Each of the eight sections of the Wisdom of Jesus ben Sirach begins with a poem in praise of Wisdom, and ends with eulogies to biblical heroes. Following the style of the Book of Proverbs, Sirach seeks to instill a love of Wisdom in his readers, and to help them translate that love into a life of moderation rooted in ethical and moral precepts. Fearful that the book would compete with Proverbs, and certain of its late authorship, the Rabbis did not include the book in the Hebrew Canon, although they quoted from it liberally. The early Christian Church did consider the book canonical, however, calling it in the Latin Vulgate Bible *Ecclesiasticus*, "the Church's Book."

The Wisdom of ben Sirach is a theologically conservative text, finding no need to wrestle with the problem of evil and suffering, as did Kohelet and Job, and placing its faith in the righteousness of God's deeds. God rewards the good, and punishes the wicked. While some books from this period begin to speak of an afterlife, Sirach does not. At death everyone goes to *Sheol,* the home of the dead. Immortality is through one's children and reputation only.

While Sirach speaks of Wisdom as a powerful and erotic woman, his advice to his students (for whom this book may have been written) treats actual women with patriarchal condescension.

At the heart of Sirach is a new understanding of the ancient Hebrew concept of the fear of God. In older Wisdom Literature, the fear of God referred to the absolute reliance of human beings on God and God's will. With Sirach God's will is known through the teachings and statutes of the Torah. Sirach equates Wisdom with Torah and in so doing seeks to legitimize the latter through the power of the former.

Sirach is also concerned with the matter of timing so central to Kohelet. Both teachers believed that you cannot know what is appropriate outside the moment. Sirach delights in posing two or more responses to various life situations without ever saying which is the preferred response. By remaining silent, he suggests that there is no way to know a priori, but that only by engaging each situation fully are you capable of discerning the right path for that moment.

Who Is She?

1 Wisdom is the first of God's creations, the Way that precedes the wayfarer, the Word that precedes the speaker. Wisdom is the Hebrew Mother, *Chochmah,* who becomes the Greek Son, *Logos,* in the Gospel According to John: "In the beginning was the Word, and the Word was with God, and the Word was God. He was in the beginning with God, all things were made through Him, and without Him was not anything made that was made" (John 1:1–3).

2 Wisdom is outside of time, embracing past and future in the timeless present. To follow Her is to taste eternity in this moment. Her statement is echoed by Jesus: "Before Abraham was I am" (John 8:58). Jesus is speaking from the perspective of Wisdom, realizing that his true self is one with Her. It is the same with you.

☐ I Am

God is my Source,
and I am His first creation.[1]

Before time—I am.
Before beginnings—I am.

There were as yet no oceans when I was born,
no springs deep and overflowing.

I am older than mountains.
Elder to the hills, the valleys, and the fields.
Before even the first lumps of clay emerged—I am.[2]

—PROVERBS 8:22–26

1 Here is Chochma as Tao:

Something mysteriously formed,
Born before heaven and earth.
In the silence and the void ...
It is the mother of ten thousand things.
I do not know its name;
I call it Tao.

—*Tao Te Ching*, 25

All things flow from Her, arise in Her, embody Her as a wave embodies the ocean. You are Her; it is only arrogance that blinds you to the fact. To know Her is to know yourself. To know yourself is to know the world, Her children, as your siblings.

I Was There

When God set the heavens in place—I was there.
When God fixed the sea's horizon—I was there.
When God made firm the sky and set the fountains
that feed the sea;
When God bound the ocean with shore,
and the sand with sea—I was there.[1]

—PROVERBS 8:27–29

1 Wisdom is not aloof. She is a player, a dancer, a celebrator of life, and the One who manifests it. She is both a source of delight and delight itself. To be wise is to delight in creation. To de-light, to be "of light," this is the gift Wisdom offers you. It is not something you lack, but something to which you are blind. To walk the way of Wisdom is to become transparent to the Light that is your very being.

God's Delight

I was God's confidant and architect,
a source of endless delight,
playing before Him without ceasing,
rejoicing in creation,
delighting in humankind.[1]

—PROVERBS 8:29–31

1 To live with attention is to be present to what is happening. Wisdom is present now. Wisdom is witness to the present; the wise act in accord with it.

2 Wisdom is like the ocean's current. You may choose to swim against it, but the effort is exhausting and you will drown. Swim with the current, however, and the sea will support and propel you. Wisdom is the current of God: Swim with Her and you align with Him.

3 In the Hebrew Scriptures the phrase "fear not" appears no less than 118 times! To be without fear is what it is to be in tune with Divine Wisdom. Fear arises from lack of trust. To embrace Wisdom is to know that you are supported, even if you do not understand what may be happening at the moment.

4 When you rule without fear, you rule without arrogance. Without fear you are naturally kind, just, humble, and wise.

☐ True Counsel

I live with attention.
attaining knowledge and foresight.[1]

The wonder of God erases evil,
and I despise pride, arrogance, evil, and deceit.[2]

I am true counsel and resourcefulness.
I am right understanding and fearlessness.[3]

Through Me kings reign kindly,
and lawmakers pass just laws.
Through Me princes rule lightly,
and judges decide without bias.[4]

—PROVERBS 8:12–16

1 Wisdom does not play hard to get. Her natural inclination is to love those who love Her, and to reveal Herself to those who seek Her. So often you excuse laziness by claiming Wisdom is too demanding. And yet all She asks of you is love. "Seek and you will find" (Matthew 7:7). The seeking is the finding. Loving is being loved. She is waiting for you. Why do you hesitate?

2 Only Wisdom, born before time, can outlast the ravages of time. No thing is permanent, yet She is not a thing, but the Way of things. Wisdom endures not because She is eternal, but because She is timeless.

3 Wisdom is the Way of right action, the path of just deeds. Right action is action that honors self and other, that uplifts the fallen, and defends the powerless. Just deeds are those that heal rather than harm, that serve the whole as well as the part. When you look at your doings in the world, are you walking with Wisdom?

4 What is of lasting value? Only Wisdom Herself. Her gift is Herself. There is nothing more you need.

□ Wisdom's Gift

I love those who love Me, and show Myself to all
who seek Me.[1]
I am true abundance, enduring prosperity.[2]
My fruit surpasses the finest gold.
My produce is superior to the choicest silver.
I walk the way of righteousness, the path of justice.[3]
I bless My lovers with wealth and fill their treasuries
with timeless things.[4]

—PROVERBS 8:17–21

1 Everlasting life is not to be mistaken for endless living. Wisdom was present before the creation of time and is Herself timeless. The Way of Wisdom leads you out of time and into the timeless present.

2 The Way of Wisdom is the way of pleasantness and peace. This is not to say that you will not encounter sorrow and strife, but that your response to misfortune is pleasantness and peace. Responding with pleasantness is responding from spaciousness, realizing that you are greater than what you witness, and capable of embracing it even as you transcend it. Responding with peace *(shalom)* is responding from wholeness *(shalem)*, knowing that self and other go together like convex with concave.

3 Wisdom is a Tree of Life only if you hold on to Her. It is your connection to Wisdom that matters. Cleaving to Wisdom means embracing the real that preexists and permeates creation. It is finding the order in the midst of chaos.

The Way

She is the way to everlasting life, true wealth,
and honor.[1]
Her way is pleasant, and all Her paths are peace.[2]
She is a Tree of Life to those who embrace Her, and
those who unite with Her find happiness.[3]

—PROVERBS 3:14–18

1 Wisdom is not separate from creation; She is the order of creation. She is the grain of wood, the currents of wind and sea. Everything rests on a metaphysical order, a principle that patterns all reality. While the world you encounter is impermanent, the principle of Wisdom is timeless. To know Wisdom is to know the current in the midst of the chaos.

Think of Her as you might probability theory. Any given throw of the dice is a matter of chance, yet over time a pattern emerges. There is a guiding principle that orders even that which appears as random. This guiding principle is Chochma. The extent to which you fixate on any one throw is the extent to which you are lost in chaos. As you step back and see the pattern, you are free to engage the game with equanimity.

Divine Order

Wisdom is the earth's foundation,
and understanding the sky's pillar.
She is the divine order patterning all creation,
from the ancient oceans to this morning's dew.[1]

—PROVERBS 3:19–20

1 Here again is a parallel with the Tao:

The valley spirit never dies;
She is woman, primal mother.
Her gateway is the root of heaven and earth.
She is like a sheer veil, translucent, almost transparent.
Use Her; She will never fail.

—*Tao Te Ching*, Chapter 6

Wisdom arises in God, and is the gateway to God. She is the foundation of all things, and the Way of all things. Wisdom is both timeless and timely, open to you now and capable of lifting you to eternity. She is the center that holds the periphery, just as the spokes of a wheel share a single hub (*Tao Te Ching*, Chapter 11).

□ Linking Each to All

She arises in God,
and is with Him forever . . .

Established before beginnings,
She transcends time.

She is God's word, a fountain of understanding;
Her ways are timeless, linking each to all,
and all to One.[1]

—Wisdom of Jesus ben Sirach 1:1–5

1 God is the Source and Substance of all things. Wisdom is the first of those things. Wisdom is the way God lays out the foundation of creation. She is the field from which all life springs.

2 What a wonderful image: Wisdom is poured out on creation. She is both the field and the rain that nurtures the field. And just as rain falls on all, so too Wisdom. You do not deserve Her; you do not earn Her. You simply receive Her. And yet …

3 She is with you according to your ability to know Her. It is as if you were begging for pennies in the street without realizing that your pockets were stuffed with hundred dollar bills. Your love of God and your ability to know Wisdom are connected. Knowing Wisdom is the way you love God, and loving God is the way you know Wisdom.

Poured Out

Who knows the root of Her?
Who fathoms Her subtleties?
There is only one so wise and so wondrous—God.[1]
He created Her and saw Her true nature.
God gave Her life and poured Her out
upon all creation.[2]
She is with you according to your ability to know Her;
For God has given Her to all who love Him.[3]

—WISDOM OF JESUS BEN SIRACH 1:6–10

1 Again, images of water are used to hint at the nature of Wisdom. She is poured out, she falls like mist, she rises like clouds. Like water, Wisdom is yielding, and yet, like water,

She is capable of wearing down the hardest stone. She holds sway not by attacking but by embracing.

The highest good imitates water,
giving life to all without struggle or striving.
She flows in places you dismiss and in this is like the Tao.

—*Tao Te Ching*, Chapter 8

There is no struggle in Wisdom's way. She does not exert Herself, but simply is Herself. When you act in accordance with Wisdom, you act without coercion. You act in sync with the current of the moment, engaging *what is* to nurture *what can* be.

God's Breath

I am the breath of the Most High,
blanketing the earth like mist,
filling the sky like towering clouds.

I encompass distant galaxies,
and walk the innermost abyss.
Over crest and trough,
over sea and land,
over every people and nation
I hold sway.[1]

—WISDOM OF JESUS BEN SIRACH 24:3–6

1 Time and beginning are simultaneous. Hebrew Genesis says, *Bereshit bara Elohim,* which English Genesis most often renders as *In the beginning God created* (Genesis 1:1). This is a misreading of the Hebrew. A more precise translation would be, *By means of beginning God created.* Creation is the stuff of beginnings. There is no beginning unless there is something that begins.

Wisdom is said to have been created before beginnings. This shows the limits of language, for in fact this cannot be. If She is created, then there is a beginning. What, then, is this Wisdom who was created before the things of creation? She is the pattern of creation, the Way of God's unfolding from eternity into time.

□ Timeless

Before time,
at the beginning of beginnings,
God created Me.
And I shall remain forever.[1]

—Wisdom of Jesus ben Sirach 24:9

1 Wisdom is the Mother of quality as well as quantity. Wisdom is the Mother of the metaphysical as well as the physical. Wisdom is not only the Mother of the rose, but the Mother of the delight that arises when you smell one.

2 Wisdom is a gift to all God has named. The named are the seemingly separate things of the natural world. Until a thing is named, it is undefined and not fully alive. In Hebrew the root of the words "speak," "word," and "thing" is the same: *dvr.* Until the word is spoken, until the thing is addressed, it does not truly exist. Wisdom is the ability to reverse the process, to speak the name in such a way as to return to the silence of God that preceded it.

Mother Wisdom

I am the Mother of true love,
wonder,
knowledge, and
holy hope.[1]
Beyond time, I am yet given to time,
a gift to all My children:
to all that He has named.[2]
—Wisdom of Jesus ben Sirach 24:18

1 Wisdom cannot be contained, and that which cannot be contained cannot be known completely. You can only know what you can objectify. Yet Wisdom is the ground out of which you come, and cannot be separated from your self and made into an object. You can no more know Her than your nose can smell itself or your ear can hear itself. Wisdom is not a thing you can know, but a Way you can follow:

> *Regarding your home, live close to the earth;*
> *Regarding meditation, delve deep into the heart;*
> *Regarding relationships, be gentle and kind;*
> *Regarding speech, be true;*
> *Regarding power, be just;*
> *Regarding career, be competent;*
> *Regarding action, be in tune with time and season.*
>
> —*Tao Te Ching*, Chapter 8

The way to follow Wisdom is to surrender narrow mind to spacious mind—the mind that knows to the knowing itself. In this way you end the tyranny of words and see what is *(choach mah)* without the filter of how you so desperately wish things to be.

Deeper Than the Abyss

The first human did not know Wisdom fully,
nor will the last ever fathom Her.
For Her mind is more spacious than the sea,
Her counsel more deep than the great abyss.[1]

—Wisdom of Jesus ben Sirach 28:29

1 You cannot define Wisdom, you can only imitate Her.

@ *Intelligent:* Hone your mind to keenly observe what is; *Holy:* Cultivate a heart that is transparent to what is; *Unique:* Realize that you are a precious and unrepeatable manifestation of God; *Subtle:* Learn to act without coercion; *Flowing:* Cut with the grain, tack with the wind; *Transparent:* Cleanse your self of selfishness; *Pure:* Cleanse your mind of drama; *Distinct:* Honor yourself and your uniqueness; *Invulnerable:* Be like water, yielding while embracing; *Good*: Work for the welfare of self and other; *Keen:* Learn to distinguish between truth and propaganda; *Irresistible:* Cultivate integrity and trustworthiness; *Gracious:* Make room for others; *Humane:* Treat all people with respect; *Faithful:* Say what you mean and do what you say; *Sure:* Rest in the Way; *Calm:* Love what is; *All-powerful:* Stop playing God and realize God is playing you; *All-seeing:* Observe the Way as well as the thing; *Available:* Be willing to share what you know and what you do not know.

Wisdom's Traits

What is Wisdom?
She is intelligent, holy, unique, subtle,
flowing, transparent, and pure;
She is distinct, invulnerable, good,
keen, irresistible, and gracious;
She is humane, faithful, sure, calm,
all-powerful, all-seeing, and
available to all who are intelligent, pure,
and altogether simple.[1]

—WISDOM OF SOLOMON 7:22–23

1 Wisdom is the subtle essence of all things. The world you encounter appears in many forms; She is the formlessness that makes form possible. Think of water: Its form may be ice, snow, rain, dew, river, stream, ocean, fog, or steam. Wisdom is the wetness of them all.

2 Impurity is ignorance: seeing less than the truth; seeing the form and not the matrix out of which form arises. Impurity only makes sense in contrast to purity; Wisdom predates them both. Just as impurity cannot take hold of Her, neither can purity. Nothing takes hold of Wisdom, for Wisdom holds all things.

3 The Mirror of God reflects all things and is none of them. She reflects whatever is: good and bad, hope and horror. Wisdom is not one thing or another, but the Way to deal with all things in their time.

God's Spotless Mirror

She is the mobility of movement;
She is the transparent nothing that pervades all things.[1]
She is the breath of God,
a clear emanation of Divine Glory.
No impurity can stain Her.[2]

She is God's spotless mirror
reflecting eternal light,
and the image of divine goodness.[3]
—WISDOM OF SOLOMON 7:24–26

1 All things are done through Her and yet She transcends all things. Wisdom is not reducible to anything; She encompasses and embodies everything. A flower is not Wisdom, but flowering is; Wisdom is the doing of God, and God is the Source and Substance of all things.

2 This is what Wisdom can make of you: a friend and prophet of God. A friend of God is one who dwells in Wisdom. A prophet of God is one who shows others how to do the same. To dwell in Wisdom is to see the ground from which all things come. To see the ground is to open yourself to what is rather than what you desire. Opened to what is, you engage the Way of things in this very moment. Things arise from the conditions that precede them, but options are always present. The prophet works with the current embedded in the conditions to nurture justice rather than injustice, compassion rather than cruelty.

Doer of All Things

Although She is one,
She does all things.
Without leaving Herself
She renews all things.[1]
Generation after generation She slips into holy souls,
Making them friends of God, and prophets;
for God loves none more than they who dwell with
Wisdom.[2]

—Wisdom of Solomon 7:27–28

1 Wisdom yields to nothing because there is no thing outside of Her to which She can surrender. Yet the Way of Wisdom is yielding. She cannot yield because She is yielding itself.

2 What is to your benefit? To be wise, to immerse yourself in the Way of Wisdom. Wisdom's desire is for you; She wants what is best for you, and that is for you to embrace Her. What keeps you from Her embrace? You own arrogance:

One who overreaches falls.
One who races tires.
One who exaggerates is a fool.
One who is pompous is ridiculed.
One who over-promises achieves little.
One who self-promotes quickly fades.

—*Tao Te Ching*, Chapter 24

Universe's Guide

She is more beautiful than the sun,
And the constellations pale beside Her.

Compared to light, She yet excels it.
For light yields to dark,
while She yields to nothing.[1]
She stretches mightily throughout the cosmos,
and guides the whole universe for its benefit.[2]

—WISDOM OF SOLOMON 7:29–8:1

1 Does God need a partner? God partners with Wisdom the way thought partners with language. Without language you could not know your own thoughts. Language provides a means for meaning. Without Wisdom God could not be known. Wisdom provides a means for God-realization. Wisdom is the grammar that orders speech. Without Her there would be only gibberish.

Judaism says that you are to partner with God in the work of *tikkun*, repairing the world with justice, kindness, and humility. You become God's partner to the extent that you become intimate with Wisdom. As you take up Her Way and embody Her teaching, you become what She is, God's partner.

God's Partner

She honors Her noble birth
by living with God Who loves Her.
She is an initiate in divine knowledge,
and a partner in all God's works.[1]

—Wisdom of Solomon 8:4

1 Wisdom is the underlying order that governs the seeming chaos of life. Know Her well and you can discern that order; discerning the order you can predict the future—not the details but the general pattern. Knowing the pattern allows you to work with the conditions that create that pattern. Working with the conditions frees you from being at their mercy, and offers you the opportunity to shift the unfolding future to the benefit of self and others.

2 Words, no less than molecules, follow a hidden order. We say one thing and often imply another. Wisdom reveals the meaning as well as the message of what you hear. To know Her is to listen to what is intended as well as what is said.

3 Knowing what is to come means that Wisdom makes clear the direction of life at any given moment. Kohelet tells us that everything has its time and purpose. The purpose of a thing ripens over time. Wisdom reveals the nature of this ripening process so that you can act at the precise moment to effect the greatest good with the least effort.

Solver of Puzzles

She knows the past,
and predicts the future;[1]
She understands the subtleties of speech
and the solution to puzzles.[2]
She divines signs and wonders,
and knows what is to come.[3]
—WISDOM OF SOLOMON 8:8

1 Love is natural to life. Its allure is stronger than death, meaning that despite knowing that all relationships must end, we enter into them anyway. Wisdom's Way is not to do away with love, but to make Her the supreme object of your love.

God's Beloved

I am my Beloved's,
and His desire is for Me.
Come, Beloved,
let us flee into the open and
dwell in the villages.
Let us run early to the vineyards
and see if the vine has flowered,
if its blossoms have opened,
if the pomegranates are in bloom.
There I will give My love to You.[1]

—Song of Songs 7:11–13

1 Desire, too, is natural to life. It is a raging fire that cannot be extinguished. The Way of Wisdom is not to do away with desire, but to cultivate the strength to withstand desire rather than be buffeted about by it. Her Way is the way of the Burning Bush: to burn and yet not be consumed.

2 Love is what unites all beings in Being. Love is what unites God and Wisdom. Love and the power to love are the keys to embracing Wisdom and Her Consort. There is nothing more powerful than this attraction. It is the gravity of the soul that holds all creation together. This love is beyond desire, beyond attachment and addiction. This love is of the nature of things. Even if God offered all He had, meaning all that is, still love transcends.

Power of Love

Place Me as a seal upon Your heart,
like a cuff on Your arm.
For love is fierce as death,
desire as inevitable as the grave.[1]
Its arrows are fire,
a raging hungry flame.
Great rivers cannot quench love,
nor floods drown it.
If You offered all You had for love,
still Your offering would be scorned.[2]

—SONG OF SONGS 8:6–7

Where Is She Found?

1 Your life is so noisy. The clamor of the street outweighed only by the clamor in your mind. And it is all the same noise: "I want, I need, I hunger, I ..." And yet above it all Wisdom can be heard. Do not pretend to deafness; admit that you just don't want what She has to offer.

Why do you cling to cynicism and folly? Because it protects you from having to admit to your own limitations. You can pretend to be above the fray, when in fact you are the source of it. Your mind is sickened by the disease of want. You imagine that there is something you lack, and the lack is killing you. But it is only in your imagination. The truth is She is waiting for you, calling to you, longing for you. It is your indifference that separates you from Wisdom. You hide behind not caring because you care so much you fear it will kill you. Surrender your façade of callousness and let Her embrace you completely.

Wisdom Calls

Wisdom shouts aloud in the street,
Her voice trumps the tumult of the market:
How long will you cling to cynicism and folly?
How long will you dull your minds with foolishness?
You are indifferent to My words,
yet I will speak My mind, and share My thoughts ...[1]

—PROVERBS 1:20–23

1 The fruit of desire is desire. There is no end to it: "The eye is never sated nor the ear made full" (Ecclesiastes 1:8). You imagine that the next thing will bring you the happiness you seek, yet it is the very seeking after happiness that is the cause of your dis-ease. Seeking happiness and being happy are mutually exclusive. As long as you seek, you cannot find. Seeking precludes finding. Finding happiness is being happy here and now with whatever is happening in and around you. This is the counsel you reject: Stop seeking! This is the direction you refuse: Be present! Pay attention to Wisdom and your desires will not cease, but the compulsion to fulfill them will.

☐ Listen to Me

If you hate knowledge and spurn Wisdom;
if you reject My counsel and refuse My direction,
you have nothing but the bitter fruit
of your own desires,
the barren hope of your own schemes.
Your recklessness will kill you,
Your desires will strangle you.

Listen to Me and My words will protect you;
heed Me and you can face your strongest desires
with calm.[1]

—PROVERBS 1:24–33

1 Wisdom is not silent, but you must become silent if you expect to hear Her. She calls above the din, but the din is of your own making, and your natural response is to increase the noise. The noise is your narrow mind, the relative self of ego, incessantly chanting its mantra: "I, me, mine." As long as you focus on this, you cannot hear Wisdom at all.

Wisdom stands above the desolate peaks and busy highways, but you focus on them. Just as your ears are clogged with the din of self, your eyes are trapped by the extremes of desolation and busyness. You have to free yourself from the distractions of self and selfishness.

2 The prize on which your eyes are focused is glittering baubles of gold and silver. Somehow you have been convinced that to be is to buy, and to buy is to be happy. Wisdom offers you an alternative. You cannot buy Her. She is free for the taking but the taking costs you everything you think you know.

Wisdom Is Not Silent

Wisdom is not silent;
She boldly raises Her voice above the din.
She stands upon the most desolate peak,
and the busiest highway,
at every intersection, gate, and doorway:[1]

Listen to Me, all of you!
Listen to Me, for I speak of noble things.
Truth comes from My lips;
My words are just and simple.
Reason and understanding will show you
the rightness of My words.
Accept Me rather than silver and fine gold.
For I surpass rubies; nothing equals the gift I offer you.[2]

—PROVERBS 8:1–11

1 There are only two kinds of people: the simple and the foolish. The simple see what is and act in accordance with it. They are the trimtabbers who have mastered the art of effecting great change through subtle movements in conscience and consciousness.

Fools race after the tangible goods of life and find themselves exhausted by the race. Afraid that they have not grabbed enough, they are too tired to reach for more. Their goal is not to be but to have.

The simple heed the call of Wisdom, "Enter here!" *Here* is the place you happen to be moment to moment. The foolish have to be enticed; the simple need only be invited.

The wondrous thing is that Wisdom is available to both. Being a fool is no obstacle to finding Wisdom. The love of Wisdom for Her children, simple and foolish, is absolute. She may be angry with the way we choose to live, but She never closes Her door to those who choose to dine with Her.

Enter Here

Wisdom's house stands firm on many pillars,
It is strong and shall not fall.
Within She prepares a fine meal,
sweetens Her wine with water,
and sets the table with great care.

She sends Her maids to the towers and rooftops
to shout Her invitation:
To the simple: "Enter here!"
To the foolish: "Eat My food, drink My wine.
Give up your folly, and live;
walk in the way of understanding."[1]

—PROVERBS 9:1–6

1 Wisdom is not without passion. Her desire is to be your lover, and share Her bed with you. What is Wisdom's bed? Discernment: the capacity to see what is and to act in harmony with it.

Living with Wisdom is acting without coercion. There is no need to force anything, for you have learned how to work with everything. The Way of Wisdom is like the sailor who tacks with the wind. She does not fight the current of air or water, but learns how to use what is to go where she desires.

When Wisdom finds you have left Her bed and lost your way, She seeks you out. She is not passive but active. She not only waits for your return but wanders in hopes of finding you and showing you the way home. All you have to do is stop hiding!

□ Seek the One

Upon my couch at night
I sought My beloved—
I searched, but found him not.
I must rise and roam the town,
through the streets and through the squares;
I must seek the one I love.[1]

—SONG OF SONGS 3:1–2

1 Wisdom isn't anywhere; She is everywhere. She cannot be found because She cannot be lost. She is not one thing, but the Way of all things. Just as you cannot separate the ocean from its current, the wind from its circuit, the wood from its grain, so you cannot separate Wisdom from the world.

Wisdom is not a thing to be found, but a Way to be lived. This is why She cannot be bought or bartered for. Wisdom is free. She is with you already. There is no one to be and nowhere to go other than who you are and where you are right at this very moment. Simply silence the noise of self and hear Her calling to you.

□ Where Is She Found?

Where is Wisdom found?
Where is the source of understanding?

You cannot set a price on Her;
She is not bought, sold, or bartered for.

The deep says, "She is not in me";
The sea says, "I do not posses Her."

She cannot be traded for gold,
nor swapped for silver.
The purest gold cannot secure Her.
Neither can precious onyx or sapphire …
A pouch of Wisdom is better than a sack of rubies.[1]

—Job 28: 12–19

1 Wisdom is how God "fixed the weight of the wind, and set the volume of the sea." Wisdom is the way seasons come and go, rains fall and cease, thunderstorms arise and fade away. Wisdom is not a way but the Way: the Way a rosebush roses and an apple tree apples. She is the Way a baby gurgles and takes his first steps. She is the Way the *I* emerges from the darkness of sleep and the Way it melts into the darkness of death.

Science is the study of Wisdom, though scientists may not think so. Physics studies the Wisdom of quanta; and astronomy the Wisdom of quasars. Biology studies the Wisdom of cells; and psychology the Wisdom of minds. When a scientist says, "I have peered into the mystery and there is no God in it," he has imagined a god separate from the world and has looked right past the true God who is the world. Wisdom is the Way God is God in the world science examines.

God Knows Her

Where is Wisdom found?
Just where is the source of understanding?

She is hidden from the eyes of the transient.
Even the highest soaring birds cannot see Her.
Destruction and Death say,
"We have heard only rumors."

God understands the way to Her;
He knows Her source.
God sees to the ends of the earth,
and observes all that is manifest.

When God fixed the weight of the wind,
and set the volume of the sea;
When God set the times of rain,
and plowed a path for thunderstorms,
God saw Her and gauged Her.
God measured Her and searched Her out.[1]

—JOB 28:19–27

1 Can a molecule escape from its cells, or can cells escape from their atoms? Can a paragraph escape from its sentences, or a sentence exist apart from its words? Everything is a process of embracing and going beyond. And this process is Wisdom.

You cannot escape Wisdom; you can only ignore Her. Wisdom is God manifest in the world you encounter moment to moment. She is the Way God is God in the dimensions of body, heart, mind, soul, and spirit.

Wisdom is the One who holds the many. She knows light and dark as we know convex and concave. The two are really one, for neither can exist without the other. All opposites are in fact complementary; each goes with the other: in with out, up with down, black with white, good with evil—there are no opposites except in your own mind. This is the trap of ignorance from which Wisdom releases you. The war of opposites is over and the dance of partners begins.

☐ No Escape

Where can I escape from Your spirit?
Where can I flee from Your presence?
If I ascend to heaven, You are there.
If I descend into Sheol, You are there.
If I take wing at dawn and come to rest
on the western horizon,
Even there Your hand will guide me;
Your right hand will hold me close.
If I say, "Darkness will conceal me,
and night will hide me from You,"
Dark is not dark for You; night is as bright as day;
darkness and light are the same.[1]

—PSALM 139:7–12

1 Wisdom manifests in you, as you. Could you beat your heart if it stopped beating on its own? Do you know how to grow hair, or even lift a finger? Do you know how to cleanse your blood through your liver? Do you know how to digest food and eliminate waste? You imagine that you do these things, but in fact they are done without your conscious attention. Otherwise everyone would die in their sleep, for during sleep there is no you to do anything.

2 You are intimate with Wisdom. She has known you from the beginning. You cannot hide from Her. On the contrary, you can take refuge in Her. This is what She offers you. You do not have to earn Her love, or be other than you are. No pretense with Her; She knows you and loves you for who you are—Herself.

Before the *I*

You created my inmost parts;
weaving me together in my mother's womb.
I thank You for that,
for I am awesomely and wondrously made.
Your work is subtle and steeped in wonder;
I know it well.[1]
My body was not hidden from You:
You gave me shape in secret recesses of the womb,
You knit me whole in the depths of the earth.
Your eyes saw my unformed limbs;
and You knew the deeds I could do
even before there was an *I* to do them.[2]

—PSALM 139:13–16

1 Wisdom desires you even more than you desire Her. There are no losers in the quest for Wisdom: Her lovers all find Her. Where do you look? Everywhere you happen to be. She is right there waiting for you. She rushes to reveal Herself to you in the midst of your life.

The biggest obstacle to finding Wisdom is realizing that She isn't hiding. You are so accustomed to the idea of a spiritual journey, a religious quest, that you imagine you have to do something and go somewhere to find Her. On the contrary, She comes to you. It is so easy that you imagine it is too easy and therefore it cannot be true.

The challenge is to be simple. There is a free lunch! As long as you are dining with Wisdom.

Wisdom Awaits You

Wisdom shines without dimming.
All who love Her, see Her;
All who desire Her, embrace Her.

She rushes to reveal Herself to those
who yearn for Her;
No matter how early you arise to find Her,
She is already waiting for you at the gate.[1]

—WISDOM OF SOLOMON 6:12–14

1 Surrendering to Wisdom is the Way of Wisdom. Rest your thoughts in Her. This is not the same as erasing your thoughts, or emptying the mind, or putting an end to thinking. Thinking is to the mind as breathing is to the lung and beating is to the heart. You cannot stop thinking; you can only cease to chase after thoughts. Wisdom does not say, Stop thinking. She says, Rest your thoughts in Me and do not be distracted by them.

You rest your thoughts in Wisdom when you allow thoughts to come and go without desire or aversion. When you cling to some thoughts and flee from others, you are no longer at rest, and certainly not at rest in Wisdom. Thoughts come and go, feelings arise and fade away: This is what the mind does. Don't seek to change it, but don't pay it more attention than it deserves. Allow things to rise and fall of their own accord, for that accord is Wisdom.

☐ Resting in Wisdom

Resting your thoughts on Her—
this is perfect understanding.
Staying mindful of Her—
this is perfect calm.
She embraces those who are ready for Her,
revealing Herself in the midst of their travels,
meeting them in every thought.[1]

—WISDOM OF SOLOMON 6:15–16

What Does She Teach?

1 To listen you must first be silent. When you are silent, the narrow mind, the small self of thought and language, melts into the spacious self of clarity and compassion. To be mindful is to be present. When you are present, the distracted self recedes and the greater self emerges. With this comes Wisdom, joy, and happiness. With this comes an end to cynicism and doubt, for these are simply stories you tell yourself about what is happening when you are afraid to simply be present to what is happening. Cynicism and doubt are hideouts from reality. If you wish to find Wisdom, step out of hiding.

Find Me

Listen to Me:
Follow Me and be happy.
Practice My discipline and grow wise.
Abandon cynicism and doubt.

I bring joy to those who listen;
I bring happiness to those who are mindful of Me …

Find Me and find life.
Find Me and find grace.
Turn your back on Me and choose death.[1]

—PROVERBS 8:32–36

1 Turning, change, impermanence—these are the simple truths Wisdom reveals; nothing magical, nothing mysterious, nothing other than the ordinary. There is no point to life; life is the point. There is nothing to gain from living; living is its own reward.

This is what Wisdom shows you. Do not seek some meaning separate from the moment. Do not race after notions of permanence and immortality. Do not ask for more than what is, for what is exhausts all notions of more and less.

You want your life to have meaning beyond itself. But all your striving after more leaves you exhausted and incapable of appreciating the gift of what is.

Cycles

The words of Kohelet, son of David, king in Jerusalem.
Utter emptiness, said Kohelet, utter transience!
What lasting value is there in all you earn
under the sun?

Birth and death,
sunrise and sunset,
northwinds and south—
cycles upon cycles and nothing new emerges.

All rivers pour into the sea, yet the sea is never full;
and the streams themselves continue flowing.
Cycles exhaust those who count them;
there is no way to list them all.[1]

—ECCLESIASTES 1:1–8

1 Why does the eye never tire of seeing? Because it never clings to what it sees. Why does the ear never tire of hearing? Because it does not hold on to what it hears. The eye sees and the ear hears and the nose smells and the tongue tastes and the fingers touch, and none of them clings to anything. Only narrow mind clings; only narrow mind treasures memory over the moment and reduces the future to an imitation of the past. Narrow mind is made of memory and lives in the past. The present threatens it by its very freshness. The present cannot be imitated, and that is why narrow mind cannot grasp it.

2 There is nothing new under the sun. There is nothing new because there is nothing old. *New* implies *old* and there is neither in the present. Everything arises together in the eternal now. Narrow mind is forever cloaking the present in the past. Spacious mind is content to be present to what is in the moment.

Nothing New

The eye never tires of seeing,
nor the ear of hearing.[1]
The future imitates the past;
time is not a line but a circle;
there is nothing new beneath the sun![2]
For what seems new now is but the old forgotten,
and what will seem new tomorrow is
but today unremembered.

—ECCLESIASTES 1:8–11

1 Unhappiness is a by-product of obsession. Obsession is clinging to what has passed. It is trying to find nourishment from the aroma of a meal rather than from the meal itself. It is feasting on wind.

2 We obsess over the past because we imagine that we can control the past. We can rewrite our memories and heal our stories. But we know we are doing this and this knowing makes healing impossible. We can no more change our past than make the straight crooked or the broken whole. All we can do with these is accept them.

3 Even knowledge fails us. The more we know, the more we know that we don't know. If this leads to humility—wonderful. But for most of us it leads to greater anxiety and a compulsion to strive for more when in fact it is the more that is killing us. Kohelet is Wisdom's sage: He is not telling us to abandon Wisdom, but to be wise; not to make of Her another object of desire, but to be with Her as with a lover who freely gives Her love to you.

Feeding on Wind

I, Kohelet, was king in Jerusalem over Israel.
I devoted my mind to Wisdom, to investigate
all we do under the sun.
An unhappy business, this life that
we mortals obsess about!
I watched all that is done beneath the sun,
and I found it as senseless as feeding on wind.[1]

A twisted thing cannot be made straight.
A shattered thing cannot be made whole . . .[2]

I set my mind to appraise even knowledge ...
and I learned that this too was chasing wind.
As knowledge grows, so grows anxiety:
The more you learn, the more you suffer.[3]

—ECCLESIASTES 1:12–18

1 Imagine that you are walking through a dark house at midday. The curtains are heavy and drawn tightly shut. No light enters the house, and you stumble blindly through each room. The foolish light a candle and pick their way among the shadows. The wise open the curtains and bathe the house in light, walking confidently wherever they will.

Wisdom will not rescue you from death, but She will allow you to live without fear.

Seeing Clearly

Wisdom is superior to folly
as light is superior to darkness.
The wise can see clearly
while the fool stumbles in ignorance.
And yet the same fate awaits them both!

The wise die just like the foolish.
So what advantage is there to Wisdom?[1]

—ECCLESIASTES 2:13–16

1 This is what Wisdom teaches: Life is this moment, and this moment, and this moment. Each moment is both means and end: fulfilling the conditions of the previous moment and setting the conditions for the next moment. There is nothing you need add to the moment. No story you need to spin. No *why,* just *what.*

Wisdom frees you from the obsession with *why.* Wisdom frees you for the wonder of *what. What* is the moment at hand: killing, healing, mourning, dancing, tearing, mending, and so on. Wisdom simply says that when the moment is for crying—cry! But do not cry when crying time has passed.

Each moment has its own integrity. Living with Wisdom means you live in that integrity. It doesn't mean you don't suffer; it means that you do not suffer a moment longer than necessary. It doesn't mean that you don't laugh; it means that you don't laugh a moment longer than appropriate. Wisdom reveals the truth of the moment. It is up to you to engage it.

Moments

Everything has its moment,
there is a time of ripening for everything under heaven.
Moments for birth, and moments for death;
Moments for planting and moments for reaping;
Moments for killing and moments for healing;
Moments for destroying and moments for creating;
Moments for crying and moments for laughing;
Moments for mourning and moments for dancing;
Moments for throwing stones and
moments for piling them;
Moments for hugging and moments for shunning;
Moments for finding and moments for losing;
Moments for keeping and moments for discarding;
Moments for tearing and moments for mending;
Moments for silence and moments for speech;
Moments for love and moments for hate;
Moments for war and moments for peace.[1]

—ECCLESIASTES 3:1–8

1 Wisdom teaches you to see what is plain as well as what is hidden. Why do you need to be taught to see what is plain? Because Her seeing is different from yours. You see things reflected in the mirror of time and memory. You see *now* cloaked in *then*. This is how you make sense of things, by seeing them as echoes of memory. Wisdom teaches you to see them as they are in the moment: fleeting expressions of an infinitely expressive God. She teaches you to see without the distortion of memory.

How can you see what is hidden? By realizing the ground out of which the figure emerges. The figure is the seen, the ground is the hidden; neither can exist without the other. Wisdom teaches you to see each moment in the context of eternity. You see the tree in the context of the forest, and the forest in the context of the mountain, and the mountain in the context of the valley, and on and on until you see all in everything and everything in all. It is not that the hidden becomes manifest, or that the ground becomes figure, but that both are seen when either is seen. The whole and the part are one in the nonduality of God.

Hidden and Manifest

I learned what is both hidden and what is manifest,
for Wisdom, the fashioner of all things, taught me.[1]

—Wisdom of Solomon 7:21–22

1 A simple heart is a heart humbled by not-knowing. Even when you can see the manifest and the hidden, you only know them in a limited way. To know something is to stand outside of it. To know something is to be greater than it. The wave cannot know the ocean, the branch cannot know the tree, the note cannot know the symphony. And while it is true that the ocean can know the wave, only the observer on the shore can know them both. The observer, the witness, can see tree and branch, and hear notes and symphony. The observer is other than the observed. But there is no other in the greater reality of God. The observer is the observed, and because this is so, knowing is impossible. God can know you, for you are to God as the branch is to the tree. But God cannot know God, for there is no observer separate from God able to grasp the Divine's full dimensions. There is always the ineffable, the unknowable, even with God. And only the simple heart is capable of accepting this.

Simple Heart

If you seek to judge the earth,
first love righteousness.
Contemplate God with a good heart,
with a simple heart seek Him.
For God cannot be found through testing,
nor does He appear to those who lack trust.[1]

—Wisdom of Solomon 1:1–2

1 Deceit and exploitation go together. The ultimate deceit is to fool yourself into believing you are separate from others. With this comes the zero-sum mentality at the root of so much of the world's horror: "If I am to win, it must at the expense of another's loss." With this you have rationalized evil in the name of self-preservation. All this does is shut out Wisdom and leave you struggling in a violent world of your own making.

Test and Deceive

Wisdom cannot take root in deceit,
nor dwell in one given to exploiting others.[1]

—Wisdom of Solomon 1:4–5

1 Can a liar be separated from his lies? Is a liar who doesn't lie still a liar? You are what you do. God knows your intent, but it is your actions alone that bear consequences. Wisdom cannot make you other than you are; She can only show you who you are at this moment. To see who you are is to have the opportunity to change what you do.

Limits of Wisdom

Wisdom is kind,
but even She cannot erase
the lies from the liar.[1]

—WISDOM OF SOLOMON 1:6

1 This is what Wisdom knows: the giving and taking of God. There is no injustice in this; no sorrow or suffering. There is just the truth of it: God gives and God takes away. All you can to is receive and release. The suffering comes from refusing to receive what you do not want, and refusing to release what you do want.

The sage knows the truth of God's giving and taking. She knows that it is all from God and that the only proper response is to thank God for both what is given and what is taken away. The alternative is to add suffering on top of suffering, insisting that life be other than it is, and God other than He is. This is what the sage refuses to do.

God Gives, God Takes

Naked and empty-handed I came out
of my mother's womb,
and naked and empty-handed shall I return there.
God gives; God takes;
blessed be the Ineffable Name of God.[1]

—JOB 1:21–22

1 Where is Job's integrity? Job's wife assumes it is in his innocence. She knows that he has done nothing to deserve the horrors God is inflicting upon him. But she isn't wise. She thinks God should be just and that justice should be what she imagines it to be, and that Job should be angry.

Job isn't angry because Job is wise. Job knows that God gives and God takes, and there is nothing to be done about it. He knows that the wise response to any moment is acceptance. His integrity is in his willingness to accept what is without rancor.

Yet the sage is not passive. For even as Job accepts what is, he does not doubt his own innocence or cease in his demand that God account for His actions. It is not that the sage doesn't want to know, but that the sage will not pretend to knowing. Job waits for God to reveal the truth, and until then he will sit with his integrity intact.

Acceptance

Job sat in the ashes
and scratched his sores
with a piece of broken crockery.
Seeing her husband in such agony,
Job's wife cried out to him,
"You still keep your integrity! Curse God and die!"
Job said to her,
"Should we accept only good from God and not evil?"[1]

—JOB 2:8–10

1 Evil and sorrow are human experiences. While all beings can suffer, only humans spin a story about their suffering, either to excuse it, explain it, or challenge it. Job's wife and even more so his friends insist on some story, some explanation, to make sense of Job's condition. The integrity of their stories matters to them more than the suffering of Job. If they can keep their stories intact, they can maintain the illusion that they understand the world, and through their understanding can control their fate. If Job is guilty, they can proclaim their own innocence and avoid the creeping fear of a capricious God. If Job is innocent, however, their fragile illusions collapse, and they are left with nothing but terror. Job is not afraid of sitting without a story. He knows that suffering is natural to humanity. He knows too that our suffering is compounded when we spin a story about it. Better to sit and wait without a story than to make matters worse.

Born for Suffering

Evil is not from the earth,
nor sorrow from the ground.
Humans are born for suffering
just as sparks fly upward.[1]

—Job 5:6–7

1 Each moment is a test. The test is not in the moment; the moment is the test. Can you accept the truth of what is happening at this very moment? That is the test. The moment is what it is. Can you accept it? You got the new job or you lost it; can you accept it? Your doctor said your cancer was operable or inoperable; can you accept it? Your child survived the accident or died; can you accept it? The test is your ability to accept what is so that you can engage what is. Failing the test means failing to deal with reality.

Why does God test you? Job doesn't answer the questions he raises because Wisdom has shown him there is no *why.* Not that there is no answer, but that the question itself is wrong. Not that it is wrong to question, but that this particular question, the question *Why,* has no meaning outside the need for a story to explain simply what is.

The sage doesn't explain why things are; the sage simply engages what is. *Why* is beside the point. A stranger throws a stone at your head. You duck; you don't ask *why.* Later you may indulge in *why,* but the moment itself requires action. Why does God test you? Because it is God's nature to manifest moments of giving and moments of taking away and there is nothing that you or God can do about it.

Forever Tested

What are humans that You bother with us?
Why do You pay such close attention to what we do?
You inspect us every morning,
and test us every moment.[1]

—JOB 7:17–21

1 Inquiring into the past in order to understand the present reduces the present to a by-product of the past. What is simply reflects the inevitable culmination of what was. This is karma: The past determines the present.

Inquiring into the present reveals each moment to be the ripening of the conditions of the past, and your engagement with this ripening can be fresh and karma free.

The present moment is the field on which you engage reality. The field is the result of conditions established in the past. If you are a compulsive liar, in time your lies will catch up with you and the field on which you find yourself will reflect the lies you have told in the past. Yet how you play out the moment is not predetermined. If you choose to continue lying, then the next ripening will be filled with the consequences of your new lies. If you choose to stop lying, then the new field will reflect the new conditions and things will change. You cannot change what is; you can only choose how to engage it, and in this way influence what will be.

Yesterday's Product

Inquire into the past;
study what the ancients searched out.
You are yesterday's product.
and know nothing yourself.[1]

—Job 8:8–9

1 The beasts, the birds, the fish, the forests, the mountains, the valleys, the entirety of nature knows itself to be of God. This knowing is Wisdom. Only humans seem ignorant of Her. Genesis tells you that you are an exhalation of God (Genesis 2:7), so why do you deny it? Why do you want so desperately to be other than you are?

You are the breath of God. You are the way God is aware of God in the immediacy of your life. You are the way God feeds the hungry, clothes the naked, frees the wrongly imprisoned. You are the way God brings justice, mercy, and humility to life. But because you want to be more, you end up being less: the way God brings horror, hate, and holocaust to every corner of the globe.

God's Hand, God's Breath

Ask the animals; they will teach you.
Inquire of the birds; they will tell you.
Speak to the earth; she will inform you.
The fish of the sea, they will instruct you.
They all know that God is the Source.
In God's hand rests the life of all the living,
and the breath of all humankind.[1]

—JOB 12:7–10

1 Job is about to make a quantum leap in his experience with Wisdom. Soon God will reveal Himself and engage him in verbal combat that will reveal to Job the deepest truths. But first he must be ready. And in this passage he tells us what that readiness is: "In my flesh I see God."

"In my flesh I see God," in this affliction I see God, in this rotting I see God, in this injustice I see God. Not that God is behind it all: God is it all. Job is ready to encounter God in the midst of his suffering because he has surpassed the need to blame God for or protect God from his suffering.

In this, Job is becoming a sage. He sees Wisdom, the Divine Feminine that orders all things—even those things that bring us pain and suffering—in all things. He is beginning to glimpse in himself what God is about to reveal to him in the cosmos: There is an order even to chaos and this order is Wisdom Herself.

☐ In My Flesh I See God

I know my Redeemer lives!
God outlasts time and space!
Is my physical torment not enough?
Must my friends assail my mind
with their foolishness?
In my flesh I see God . . .[1]

—Job 19:25–26

1 Here God peppers Job with one *koan*-like puzzle after another. A koan is a question without a logical answer, a means for putting narrow mind in a double bind and thus forcing it to give way to spacious mind and a new level of awareness. Wisdom is the Puzzle Solver (Wisdom of Solomon 8:8), and these are the kinds of puzzles She teaches us to solve.

Where were you when the earth's foundations were laid? You were there! Not the narrow you that is bound by time and story, but the spacious you, the timeless you at one with Wisdom and Her God. You were there, because there is here, and then is always now.

This is what Wisdom wants to tell you: You are not who you think you are.

What You Know

Then God swallowed Job in a whirlwind, saying,
Who are you who darkens counsel
by speaking without knowledge?
Gird your loins like a warrior; I will ask
and you will answer Me!
Where were you when I laid the earth's foundations?
Speak if you have understanding ...

Have you ever commanded the day to break,
or assigned the dawn its place? ...
Have you penetrated the source of the sea,
or walked the recesses of the deep?
Have you surveyed the earth's expanse?
Tell Me what you know of these![1]

—JOB 38:1–4, 12, 16, 18, 21

1 Who can do all things? Only God. God fashions reality according to Wisdom. She is the blueprint for creation. She is the Way of the world in all its hidden and manifest parts. And God is even greater than She.

If God is greater than Wisdom, God must be greater than you. And if God is greater than you, how dare you question God! This is the conventional way of reading this passage of Scripture, but not Wisdom's way.

God is greater than Wisdom and encompasses Wisdom. God's greatness is not "other than" but "inclusive of." If God were "other than," there would be a place where God was not. God could not be infinite if God did not include you. God includes all. Nothing is "other than" to God. Nothing is outside of God. This is what God wants Job to know, and what Wisdom wishes to teach you.

Who did all these things? God. And who is God? Your truest Self.

☐ Who

Who put Wisdom in the hidden parts?
Who gave understanding to the mind?
Who is wise enough to give an account of the heavens?
Who can tilt the skies and pour out rain?[1]

—Job 38:36–37

1 The Truth is dawning on Job. He doesn't have an arm like God's; he is God's arm. He doesn't have a voice like God's; he is God's voice. You do not act like God; God acts like you. You are the way God gets "you" done.

The only response to this awakening is to clap your hands over your mouth and be silent. But the need to clap your hand over your mouth suggests that there is still something more you wish to say, and it is this "something more" that still needs to be released. This "something more" is the last vestige of your need for a story that makes sense of all of this to narrow mind. You can impose silence, but this is not yet the silence of true Wisdom.

An Arm Like God's

Job answered God, saying,
I am of little worth;
how can I reply?
I clap my hand to my mouth.
I have spoken once,
and not again;
twice, but no more.
Then God spoke to Job out of the storm, saying,
Gird your loins like a warrior;
I will ask, and you will answer Me.
Would you impugn My justice?
Would you make Me wrong, that you may be right?
Have you an arm like God's?
Can you thunder with a voice like Mine?[1]

—Job 40:3–9

1 Here is Job's full awakening. He realizes the limits of his story and knows now that he doesn't know and cannot know, for he is not other than the Knower and the known.

In the past Job heard stories and theories about God; now he sees God for himself. And this direct seeing always leads to surrendering to the silence. This direct seeing is the Way of Wisdom. It is She who calls you to investigate the nature of things. It is She who challenges you to drop your story about reality and see what is real in and of itself.

2 To surrender is to release the last story and the need for story. Without the need for story, silence arises naturally. There is no imposition of silence, no clapping of the hand over the mouth; there is simply silence arising from the lack of any need to speak. The mind becomes still. The past is let go. And in the stillness and the silence there is pure love, acceptance, and creativity. Why creativity? Because without the noise of the past distracting you from the present, you are suddenly free to engage what is rather than habitually re-create what was.

3 "Dust and ash" is a celebration not a condemnation. The sage is not ashamed of being dust and ash, but is overwhelmed by the wonder of it. The sage realizes that humans are the way dust and ash knows itself divine.

Dust and Ash

Job again answered God, saying,
I know You can do everything.
I know that nothing You imagine is beyond Your doing.
You ask,
"Who is this who obscures counsel without knowledge?"
True, I spoke without understanding
of things about which I did not know.[1]
You said to me,
"Hear now, and I will speak; I will ask, and You will inform me."
In the past I had heard You with my ears;
now I see You with my eyes.
Therefore, I surrender to the silence,[2]
knowing I am dust and ash.[3]

—Job 42:1–6

The Way of the Wise

1 You want to be embraced by Wisdom; you desire Her love as much as She desires to love you. A part of you may doubt and question; a part may seek to hide from your desire in cynicism, but at your core you want Her.

A single encounter with Wisdom is enough to lift you out of your desperately reasoned ego, and to leave you breathless with love and desire. Wisdom is not a cool intellectual exercise, but a hot embrace. Wisdom is not dispassionate, but the Way of passion.

Captured by Wisdom

You have captured my heart,
my sister, my bride.
You have captured my heart
with a single glance,
with one coil of Your necklace.
How sweet is Your love,
more intoxicating than wine!
Your perfume more fragrant than the finest spice![1]

—SONG OF SONGS 4:9–10

1 There are two kinds of immortality, the dream of endless time that is the narrow mind's hope, and the stepping out of time that is spacious mind's reality. The first is a projection of ego, fearful of its own transience. The second is a gift from Wisdom when you devote yourself to Her.

What is the devotion Wisdom requires? First, your willingness to put Her above your own egocentric hungers; second, dedication to Her discipline. Wisdom's discipline requires you to see through the façade of time and space into the infinite expanse of God, to see the grain of the moment and to cut with it and not against it. In this lies true immortality, the ability to act without coercion, to be without becoming, and to embrace the timeless present without the burden of past or future.

Immortality

The desire for instruction begins
with the love of Wisdom.
The love of Wisdom requires
devotion to Her discipline.
Devotion to Her discipline leads you
toward immortality,
and immortality brings you to God.[1]

—Wisdom of Solomon 6:17–19

1 What is the one way into life? Empty-minded. What is the one way out? Empty-handed.

Birth finds you without Wisdom; though She has known you since conception, you do not yet know Her. Though She is the way you are fashioned, you are ignorant of Her presence. Death finds you without accumulation, your hands unclenched and empty. There is nothing left over; you leave without residue.

Wisdom is the Way you move from birth to death with grace and freedom. If you make Her the treasure of your life, She will bless you with the treasures of living. If you hold Her up as a beacon, She will enlighten your mind and lighten your heart. Everything comes from Her, for She is everything's Mother and yours.

Mother Wisdom

There is but one way into life,
and one way out.
So I prayed, and understanding was given me:
I called upon God, and Wisdom came to me.

I preferred Her to scepters and thrones;
Vast wealth was nothing in comparison to Her.
Before Her, gold is like sand; silver like clay.
I loved Her above health and beauty,
and chose Her eternal radiance over the most
scintillating light.

All good things came to me with Her,
and I took joy in them because of Her,
but I did not then know She was their Mother.[1]

—WISDOM OF SOLOMON 7:7–12

1 When you are aligned with God in Wisdom, you can trust your mind and the thoughts it produces. You can act without hesitation, trusting in the Way and knowing that it is the Way of compassion and truth.

This is how you will know you are aligned with Wisdom: Your actions will be smooth and unhalting. The narrow mind acts rashly, the spacious mind acts unhesitatingly; the first acts without thinking, the second without second-guessing. The first pretends it is the second, but the results are suffused with suffering. The second pretends to nothing, and compassion arises of its own accord.

When you are one with Wisdom in God, you are one with God in Wisdom. Then you know that Father and Mother are one as well.

All Is God's

God permits me to speak without hesitation,
To trust that my thoughts are aligned with truth.
It is God who leads us to Wisdom,
And it is God who instructs the wise.
Our words and our lives are God's,
As is all Wisdom and craft.[1]

—Wisdom of Solomon 7:15–16

1 This is what the sage knows: the way of things, the Way of Wisdom who is the ordering principle of things. This knowing is not limited by labels such as *spiritual* or *material;* it encompasses both worlds and sees no boundary between them.

The sage is not the opponent of science and reason, but their champion, placing them in the larger world of God's design.

Those who pit science against spirit or spirit against science understand neither science nor spirit. The sage explores Wisdom in all Her manifestations, and transcends all categories in quest of the One who operates as each.

The Gift of Knowing

God has given me certain knowledge
of the way things are:
to know how the world was made,
and the operation of the elements.
I know a thing's beginning, middle, and end.
I understand the alternating of sun and moon,
and the turning of seasons.
The cycle of the year is known to me,
and the positions of the constellations.
The nature of living things, the passion of wild beasts,
the violence of storms, the rationalizations
of human beings,
the diversities of plants and the healing power of roots;
all things both hidden and revealed, are known to me.[1]

—Wisdom of Solomon 7:17–21

1 When you begin the Way of the sage you do so in wonder. When you complete the journey, your wonder is compounded. No matter where you travel, the world is a fierce and wondrous thing.

Each step of your journey is filled with wonder. It is how you know you are on the Path. If you investigate Wisdom and find your heart grown cold, then you know it is not Wisdom you explore but folly. Wisdom is passionate and heartfelt, giving rise to compassion and love. Falsehood weaves a life of bitterness and fear, giving rise to cynicism, anger, and despair masquerading as irony.

Wonder

The beginning of Wisdom?
Wonder!
The culmination of Wisdom?
Wonder!
The crown of Wisdom?
Wonder!
The root of Wisdom?
Wonder!
And Her branches?
Long life![1]

—WISDOM OF JESUS BEN SIRACH 1:14, 16, 18, 20

1 Wisdom is God active in time and space. She is the Way being is present in becoming. To seek Her here is to seek Him now. To find Her here is to find Him everywhere.

To serve God is to devote yourself to Wisdom: to investigate each moment, to reveal its truth, and to act in accord with it.

Love Her

Love Her and love life!
Seek Her early and be filled with joy.
Hug Her tightly and inherit glory,
and wherever you enter will be blessed.
To serve Her is to serve God.
To love Her is to be loved by God.[1]

—WISDOM OF JESUS BEN SIRACH 4:12–14

1 Wisdom will not protect you from your own folly. Nor will She reveal Herself to you all at once. So your first steps on Her Path can be confusing. You are so used to the world as narrow mind imagines it that the spaciousness She reveals to you appears unreal and frightening. If you give in to the fear and run back to folly, She will not stop you. She calls to you, but She does not coerce you.

Make room for confusion and even fear, and you will pass through both. Do not imagine Her to be one way or another; do not pretend She is limited by the straight as you are limited by the narrow. Simply stay open to what is, and in time you will see through it all to Her.

Comfort or Ruin

In the beginning Her way appears crooked,
and You are filled with fear and dread.
Her discipline is a torment,
but this is a test of your resolve.
If She can trust your intent,
and your deeds are disciplined,
then She will show you the straight way.
You will be comforted
and all secrets will be opened to you.
But if you cannot stay,
She will let you go,
and your ignorance will ruin you.[1]

—WISDOM OF JESUS BEN SIRACH 4:17–19

1 As you must make room for both the crooked and the straight, you must also make room for both shame and grace.

There are two kinds of shame. There is shame that humiliates; this is deadly. There is also shame that humbles; this is life-giving. The first leads to despair, and precludes change. The second leads to simplicity and invites change.

Everyone makes mistakes, follows dead ends, and takes detours that promise much and yield nothing. If you imagine that making these mistakes precludes you from changing course, then your imagination has doomed you. If you realize, however, that you are never lost as long as your eye remains fixed on the goal, then you will allow for error and the shame error sometimes carries; you will feel the shame and move beyond it.

Shame and Grace

Act harmoniously with each moment,
beware of evil,
and do not fear shame.
There is a false shame that leads to error,
but there is a true shame that leads to grace.[1]

—WISDOM OF JESUS BEN SIRACH 4:20–21

1 What is the detachment Wisdom counsels? It is freedom from fear. If you are detached from your own welfare, you are free from the fear of your own failure. Free from this, you are free to explore without hesitation. Detachment does not remove you from the world; it frees you to engage it more fully.

2 Impartiality is not to be mistaken for not caring, nor is it a call to deny the difference between good and evil. There is goodness, justice, compassion, and righteousness; and there is evil, injustice, cruelty, and exploitation. These are not to be confused. They are just not to be seen as separate one from the other. Good and evil, justice and injustice, compassion and cruelty, righteousness and exploitation—each goes with the other, and the sage knows this. Thus the sage does not seek to eliminate one in favor of the other, but chooses to actualize one rather than the other.

Detached Not Hidden

Be detached from your own welfare,[1]
and impartial when considering others.[2]
Do not stay silent when speech is called for,
nor abandon the world to hide in spirit.

—Wisdom of Jesus ben Sirach 4:22–23

1 The sage is not opposed to speech, nor does she overvalue silence. Each has its place and time, and the sage does what is appropriate to the moment.

The difference between the sage and the fool is in the quality of their speech and silence. The sage speaks what she knows, the fool what he desires. The sage is silent when he is unclear about the truth; the fool is silent when she is caught in a lie.

The sage admits her wrongs and corrects them; the fool is silent about his mistakes and repeats them. The sage knows the current and flows with it; the fool seeks to reshape the river to conform to his desire.

Reshape the River

The right words can point to Wisdom,
and learning can increase through speech.
Only do not speak against truth,
nor pretend to know what you do not.
Admit your mistakes, and do not reshape the river.[1]

—WISDOM OF JESUS BEN SIRACH 4:24–26

1 Falsehood and truth are the poles of Wisdom's knowledge. She knows both, but aligns Herself with the latter. She knows folly, for without it truth makes no sense. The two together allow each its individuality.

2 Rank and power are the politics of falsehood. The only way to impart falsehood is to enforce it through power. A free and reasoning mind will not believe what isn't so, but you can frighten anyone into pretending it is so.

The sage desires no rank. She is the servant who is first by being last. Her power is like water, soft and yielding yet capable of wearing away the hardest stone. Whenever you find yourself craving rank and power, know that you are in the grasp of falsehood. Stop what you are doing, and find Wisdom.

Strive for Truth

Do not apprentice yourself to fools,
nor align yourself with rank and power.[1]
Strive always for truth,
and God shall be your power.[2]

—Wisdom of Jesus ben Sirach 4:27–28

1 The Way of Wisdom, the way of the sage, is the middle way. You do not act too soon or too late, but at the precise moment when your action will have maximum impact. You do not frighten or intimidate, but stand ready to act in accord with the needs of the moment. You are aware of what is, without forcing people to be aware of you. You do not give in order to receive, or withhold in order to exploit. You give because giving is called for; you withhold because doing otherwise would cause more suffering. The key is always to know what the moment requires and to act in accord with it.

Neither Early Nor Late

Do not speak too soon,
nor act too late.
Do not rule your household like a lion,
nor your servants like a watchdog.
Do not offer your palm in order to receive,
nor tighten your fist when it is time to give.[1]

—Wisdom of Jesus ben Sirach 4:29–31

1 You cannot delay planting. You cannot rush the harvest. There is a reality to farming that is greater than your will. If you wish to succeed, you must plant when planting time is at hand, and harvest when harvest time presents itself. The sage knows this is not her doing; the fool imagines herself lord of time.

Wisdom is the Way of nature; the sage walks in accord with it. Wisdom is the Way of nurture; the sage walks in harmony with it. Wisdom is the Way of culture; the sage walks in step with it. In this way the sage brings Wisdom to bear on all things, for she is a stranger to no thing.

☐ The Right Time

Discipline yourself from childhood,
and Wisdom will accompany you through old age.
Come to Her as a farmer comes to the soil:
Plow and sow and wait for Her to arise.
Do not try too hard,
for there is a naturalness to Her coming,
and you will eat of Her fruit at the right time.[1]

—WISDOM OF JESUS BEN SIRACH 6:18–19

1 Holding back who you are is hiding. Holding back what you have is hesitation. Hiding and hesitation keep you from Wisdom.

Holding back nothing of who you are is honesty. Holding back nothing of what you have is simplicity. Honesty and simplicity are the ways to Wisdom.

When you find Her, hold her tightly. Do not let Her go, but surrender yourself to Her in perfect rest and joy. You find rest because you are no longer pretending to be what you are not. You find joy because you are no longer hoarding what you have.

□ All You Have and Are

Come to Her with all you are,
and keep Her ways with all you have.
Search and seek, and She will be found,
and when you hold Her, do not let Her go.
For in this is perfect rest and joy.[1]

—WISDOM OF JESUS BEN SIRACH 6:26–28

1 Wisdom is willing to give Herself to you. She calls to you from the rooftops and crossroads. Her desire is for you, but you must desire Her in return. She cannot force you to love Her. She will not seduce you into following Her. She is waiting for you, even pursuing you, but never coercing you.

Will you come to Her? It is up to you. Will you let yourself be taught? Will you devote yourself to Her discipline? Will you listen that you may hear Her lessons? Will you focus that you may become wise?

Wisdom's love of you is choiceless. Your love for Her must be the same.

☐ If

If you are willing, you will be taught.
If you are diligent, you will progress.
If you listen, you will learn.
If you pay attention, you will become wise.[1]

—Wisdom of Jesus ben Sirach 6:32–33

1 Wisdom is present in Her sages, and it is through them that you can find Her. Seek out Her lovers and apprentice yourself to them. Pay attention to their talk; learn their stories, puzzles, parables, and poems. Make yourself a constant guest in their midst. Do not expect them to teach you; expect only to learn as they teach themselves.

Apprentice Yourself

Stand in the company of the elders;
and apprentice yourself to the wise.

Listen closely to every discussion,
and let not the parables of understanding escape you.

Visit the sages often;
let your feet wear grooves in their walkway.[1]

—Wisdom of Jesus ben Sirach 6:34–36

1 You do not become wise all at once. There are stages, and what marks each is the lessening of ego and the expansion of grace. You begin as a narrow stream and hope to water your private garden. This is using Wisdom to better yourself. Then your stream becomes a river, too wide for your private garden and less inclined to feed the self alone. Then your river becomes a sea and from it all gardens are watered.

You know when you have arrived as a sea when you no longer labor for your self but for Self, and give Wisdom freely to all who seek it. The sea welcomes all who come to Her, and any who know Her Ways can cross Her. But the fool will fight the truth and drown in the shallowest brook.

☐ Not For Myself Alone

At first I was like a narrow stream from a river,
and as a shallow brook into a garden.
I said, I will water my best garden,
I will moisten my finest beds,
Then my brook became a river,
and my river became a sea.
In this way
I make instruction glisten in the morning,
its shimmering seen from afar.
I pour out teaching as prophecy,
and leave it for future generations.
Know this:
I do not labor for myself alone,
but for all you who seek Wisdom.[1]

—Wisdom of Jesus ben Sirach 24:30–34

1 When it comes to Wisdom, let your desire guide you. Take Her and eat of Her and do so without reserve or hesitation. She wants you to want Her, and desires to give Herself to all who hunger for Her.

To find Her and to lose Her is better than not to have found Her at all. The memory of Her love will stay with you and push you to seek Her again. There is nothing as sweet as Wisdom's love. Her taste, Her touch, Her gifts of simplicity and grace cannot be matched. And when you receive them, the narrow self is overcome with joy and the spacious self unfolds in bliss.

Come to Me

Do you desire Me?
Come to Me!
Do you crave Me?
Eat My fruit!
Even the memory of Me is sweeter than honey,
and to possess Me is sheer ecstasy.[1]

—WISDOM OF JESUS BEN SIRACH 24:19–20

1 Your desire for Wisdom is without limit. At first you hope to taste Her and be satisfied, but you cannot get enough and your hunger is never sated. At first you hope to sip Her, but a sip becomes a gulp and your thirst is never quenched. Not that She is small or dry, but that your desire grows with every bite and every swallow.

Desire is what brings you to Wisdom, but desire is not enough to be one with Her. For that, surrender is obligatory. You must give Her not only your passion but your will. Only then does She give you clarity and liberation; only then does the hunger end and the true feast begin.

□ Be Full

You who eat Me
shall yet be hungry,
and you who drink Me
shall yet be thirsty.
Only you who obey Me
shall know clarity.
Only you who align with Me
shall know simplicity.[1]

—WISDOM OF JESUS BEN SIRACH 24:21–22

1 There are fools who pretend to be sages, and sages who are mistaken for fools. Look beneath the surface and be not content with appearances.

The fool who pretends to Wisdom uses silence as a ploy, pretending to know and not say, when he does not know what to say. The sage speaks, but only when speech is necessary. Sometimes this speech is harsh: Do not mistake the sage for a coward or a pushover. Do not mistake the sage for an enabler. The sage sees the grain of the moment and lays it bare. Sometimes harsh, sometimes comforting, the moment determines what the sage says, while the fool is driven by a compulsion to manipulate self and other.

□ Silence

Not all silence is the same.
Some are silent and thought wise,
while others are despised because they speak.
Some are silent because they don't know what to say,
while others are silent because
they know when not to speak.

The wise keep quiet until the moment
for speaking is ripe.
The fool babbles without regard
to the time and season.

The babbler will be detested.
The self-proclaimed authority will be despised.[1]

—WISDOM OF JESUS BEN SIRACH 20:5–8

1 Not all who are called sages are wise. Some instruct well, and yet cannot follow their own instruction. If they do so willfully, shun them; if they do so because that is the best they can do, learn from them, but be wary of them.

Others are masters of words, but their words are empty of meaning. These serve only themselves, even if they are convinced that this cannot be so. Do not take to heart everything you hear. Wisdom is not irrational, though She may be nonrational. Wisdom is never against reason, though She may transcend reason.

2 How to tell the true sage from the false? By their fruits. If they prosper by following their teachings rather than by selling them, they are sages worthy of your loyalty and love.

☐ Sages

There are those who teach many,
yet are deaf to their own instruction.
There are others whose words are clever,
but whose meaning is false.
These shall starve,
for they are deprived of Wisdom.[1]

Those who follow their own teachings
and prosper therein,
these are trustworthy sages.[2]
—WISDOM OF JESUS BEN SIRACH 37:19–22

1 To open your ears is to listen to everything and everyone with a quiet mind. If all you hear is the echo of your own selfish chatter, you may grow clever but not wise. To incline your heart is to humble yourself before the awesome challenge of Wisdom. Do not mistake a hunger for rank and power for a desire for Wisdom.

You know you have found Her when joy, grandeur, and grace envelope you. You know you have found Her Husband when your mind grows simple, and you can see the truth of life's complexity without the imagined drama of complication.

Open Your Ears, Incline Your Heart

Open your ears to Wisdom
and incline your heart to clarity.
Call on Understanding,
a trusted Mother whose love is all you need.
Seek Her joyfully as though
She were a hidden treasure.
Only joy reveals the grandeur and grace of God.
God is unbounded Wisdom, knowledge, and insight.
Wisdom upon Wisdom, God is the foundation of truth.
Only the mindful will find God,
only the simple will know truth;
and God will grant these to you,
safeguarding the paths of justice
and protecting those who choose to walk them.[1]

—PROVERBS 2:2–8

1 When you have found your way to Wisdom, all Ways lead back to Her. When you have taken refuge in Her arms, you can be alone and never lonely. The place of Wisdom is not a place you stay, but a place that stays with you. She reveals Herself to you everywhere. So there is no need to stay anywhere. The sage is a wanderer who is never lost; your every step is both departure and arrival. The world will appear transparent to you: You will see all its doings, both foolish and wise, and you will not be deceived. You will engage the world with justice and compassion, giving and receiving without fear or hesitation.

Embracing Wisdom

When Wisdom is embraced
righteousness, justice, and fairness are known;
all paths are illumined
and you need fear no detour.
When Wisdom enters your heart
and knowledge your soul,
you will perceive the order of the universe
and never despair.
You will be rescued from your own dark inclinations,
and not even the cleverest lies will deceive you.[1]

—PROVERBS 2:9–13

1 Wisdom's love for you is unconditional. You can choose to follow Her or reject Her, and still She will love you. But Her love is not enough, for without your choosing to return that love, there is no relationship between you.

There are two paths through life, the living and the dead. The living path is Wisdom's Way; the dying path is the way of folly and wickedness. The path of the living is a refuge for life: Each step is peace, each step is healing, each step is whole and balanced. There is no destination; the journey itself is the prize.

The path of the dying is about arriving—getting somewhere other than here, for here is filled with anxiety, fear, and suffering. But there is nowhere but here, so the traveler on dying's way rushes from place to place, certain that the next place will be the last place. There is no joy in dying's way; exhaustion is its only promise.

Wisdom's Loyalty

You can, of course, forsake the light
and wander in the dark.
You can take pleasure in evil, and rejoice in clouding
the mind with words.
You can choose the crooked road or dead end,
and still Wisdom will rescue you.
You can abandon My teaching and pursue desire.
You can banish insight from your home
and open your doors to those who cannot face truth.
But as long as you choose this road,
the living path is lost to you.
Choose differently: Seek Wisdom and
walk the good path.
The upright dwell in timeless Wisdom; the
wholehearted can never be lost,
but the wicked are driven from every place
and the faithless have nowhere to call home.[1]

—PROVERBS 2:14–22

1 There is no arriving on the living path of Wisdom. There is only this step, and this step, and this step. There is no perfection on Wisdom's path, there is only perfecting. One step is not superior to another other, only more thoughtful, compassionate, just, and wise.

With every step there is something to do. Large or small, complex or simple, each moment offers you an opportunity to act. Do what you can with each opportunity. Give when giving is what is required. Take when taking is what is appropriate. There is no right action for every step, only a right action at every step. Even if your path takes you into the realms of falsehood and chaos, you can act for Wisdom and order. It matters less where you step than it does what you do when you get there.

Do What You Can

If you have the power to do good to the deserving—
do it!
If you have the means to repay a loan when asked—
do so!
If your neighbor is trusting,
be worthy of that trust.
If your neighbor is peaceable,
pick no fight with him.
If you abide among the lawless,
do not envy or imitate them.[1]

—PROVERBS 3:27–31

1 You are what you do, but what you do depends on how you think; so guard your thoughts from irrationality and falsehood. Do not shun evil thoughts; simply do not cling to them. When evil is seen to be evil, harmful to self and others, you will not do it. But if your mind is lost in false thinking, you will call evil "good" and praise yourself as you perpetuate it.

Deviating to the right or the left, letting your mind wander from truth into falsehood, is the danger; staying centered is the challenge. If you walk with a spacious mind, your feet will not lead you into temptation.

Guard Your Mind

Guard your mind more than anything you own,
for mind is the source of your reality.
Keep away from crooked speech,
and avoid clever talk.
Fix your eyes forward;
keep your gaze steady and straight.
Carefully examine the course you choose,
and all your ways will prosper.
Deviate neither to the right nor the left,
and keep your feet from evil.[1]

—PROVERBS 4:23–27

1 There was once a queen who built a palace of only one room. She sat herself at the center and invited all her subjects to meet with her. Inside the palace she had placed many mirrors that created the illusion of walls and hallways. The people became confused, wandering about the great hall blind to the queen in their midst. She also placed pouches of gold and sacks of silver throughout the room, so that as the people wandered about they would come across them and grow rich. Her people rejoiced at their good fortune, but when the pouches were all found, they tired of their search and went home, all thoughts of their queen banished from their minds. The queen was saddened that her people had abandoned their search so soon, and called to them, "Wait! I am right here! Look beyond the illusion and see me!"

Life is filled with mirrors, and from time to time you stumble onto pouches of gold. You become distracted and tired and want to rest, but the real treasure is not hidden and surpasses anything you have found. Drop all you have and heed Her call.

□ Focus

Focus on Wisdom,
and do not be distracted.
Watch the patterns of creation,
and you will awaken to grace and tranquility.[1]

—PROVERBS 3:19–22

1 Resting in God is resting in Wisdom. Wisdom does not change what is; She simply lets you see what is and act accordingly. Acting in accord with the moment, you act without coercing of self or others. Your movements are graceful and you live without hesitation or regret. At the end of the day there is nothing left undone. You sleep with a clear mind and an open heart.

Rest in God

When you know the truth
you can walk forward without stumbling.
Then you will sleep without fear;
and wake without worry,
for you rest safely in God,
and your feet do not stray from the Path.[1]

—PROVERBS 3:22–26

1 This is the Way of the wise. She is not simply *in* the world; she is *of* the world. The world is her household. She works to further kindness and cheer. She is open to knowing all there is to know, and closes her door to nothing that is true.

The sage is not a hermit or a monk, but a wife and mother, husband and father, friend and lover. There is nothing too menial or mundane, nothing beneath the calling of the wise. Rather they do everything with joy.

The Way of the Sage

A Woman of Valor, who is worthy of her?
Her value is far beyond pearls.
She guides your heart,
and through Wisdom her household flourishes.
She repays kindness with kindness
and is never driven by revenge.
She buys wool and flax,
and works cheerfully in her house.
She fills herself with Wisdom from far-off lands,
like a merchant ship laden with treasure.[1]

—PROVERBS 31:10–14

2 The sage is a servant to her servants, seeing to the needs of those she nurtures. She is wise in the ways of business. She is in tune with God and brings godliness into all her affairs. She is active, useful, engaged, and vibrant. Her hands are ready to spin thread and give alms. She never takes a superior attitude; instead, She does all things with grace.

She rises early to attend to her household,
her family, and her servants.
She plans her expenditures with care;
She buys land and plants a vineyard.
She is a tower of strength,
her arms strong and secure.
She devotes herself to what is useful;
and lets nothing snuff out her lamp.
She reaches for the spinning wheel,
and cradles the spindle in her palm.
She opens her hands to the poor,
and her arms to embrace the needy.[2]

—PROVERBS 31:15–20

3 The sage knows the times and seasons and prepares for them. She can see the coming of the cold and wraps herself and her charges in wool. She is not averse to beauty, and enjoys the good things in life.

Do not imagine that the Way of Wisdom is austere and lifeless. On the contrary, working with Wisdom allows you to engage the best life has to offer. Yet you do so lightly, knowing nothing lasts; and justly, knowing your responsibility to the welfare of self and others.

She fears no winter, for she has clothed
her household in scarlet wool.
She makes for herself glorious bedspreads;
and dresses of fine linen and purple wool.[3]

—PROVERBS 31:21–22

4 The sage is a servant-leader. She has no need to take center stage, and is content to guide those who desire power in order to keep them humble and honest.

She is industrious and compassionate. She manufactures fine goods, and sells them at a profit. There is no aspect of life that cannot be uplifted through dignity and diligence.

So often we imagine sages to be otherworldly, but the Way of Wisdom is the way of the world awake to its Source and Substance. The sage rests in God and does all things without coercion or excessive effort.

She counsels her husband
and her knowledge makes him wise among the elders.
She weaves cloth, and sells cloaks and
belts to peddlers.
She adorns herself with dignity,
and is not afraid of the truth.
Her speech is full of Wisdom,
her tongue teaches human kindness.
She anticipates the needs of her household,
and does not eat the bread of laziness.[4]

—PROVERBS 31:23–27

5 Many who look like sages are only masking their own foolishness. Do not praise everyone who is successful, for their success may have been at another's expense. Do not be duped by outward trappings. Love the sage whose life is informed by God and whose living is infused with godliness.

Each morning her children feel blessed,
her husband praises:
There are many wonderful women, but you surpass them all.
Do not be taken in by grace and beauty alone;
praise only the woman who devotes herself to God.
The way she lives is evidence of her integrity;
Her whole life is a testament to her goodness.[5]

—PROVERBS 31:28–31

Suggestions for Further Reading

Barre, M., ed. *Wisdom, You Are My Sister*. Washington, DC: Catholic Biblical Association of America, 1997.

Bergant, Dianne. *What Are They Saying about Wisdom Literature?* New York: Paulist Press, 1984.

Bloom, Harold. *Where Shall Wisdom Be Found?* New York: Riverhead, 2004.

Boström, L. *The God of the Sages: The Portrayal of God in the Book of Proverbs*. Stockholm: Coronet Books, 1990.

Bryce, Glendon E. *A Legacy of Wisdom: The Egyptian Contribution to the Wisdom of Israel*. London: Associated University Press, 1979.

Brenner, A., ed. *A Feminist Companion to Wisdom Literature*. Sheffield, UK: Sheffield Academic Press, 1995.

Brueggemann, Walter. *In Man We Trust*. Richmond: John Knox Press, 1972.

Camp, C. V. *Wisdom and the Feminine in the Book of Proverbs*. Sheffield, UK: Sheffield Academic Press, 1985.

Collins, John J. *Jewish Wisdom in the Hellenistic Age*. Louisville: Westminster John Knox Press, 1997.

Crenshaw, James. *Old Testament Wisdom: An Introduction*. Atlanta: John Knox, 1981.

Gammie, J. G., and L. G. Perdue, eds. *The Sage in Israel and the Ancient Near East*. Winona Lake, IN: Eisenbrauns, 1990.

Lang, B. *Wisdom and the Book of Proverbs: An Israelite Goddess Redefined*. New York: Pilgrim, 1986.

Mack, Burton. *Wisdom and the Hebrew Epic.* Chicago: University of Chicago Press, 1985.

McKane, William. *Prophets and Wise Men*. Philadelphia: Naperville, 1965.

Morgan, Donn. *Wisdom in the Old Testament Traditions*. Atlanta: John Knox, 1981.

Murphy, R. E. *The Tree of Life: An Exploration of Biblical Wisdom Literature*. New York: The Anchor Bible Reference Library, 1990.

O'Connor, K. M. *The Wisdom Literature*. Wilmington, DE: Michael Glazier Books, 1988.

Perdue, Leo G. *Wisdom and Creation*. Nashville: Abingdon Press, 1994.

Schroer, S. *Wisdom Has Built Her House: Studies on the Figure of Sophia in the Bible*. Trans. L. M. Mahoney and W. McDonough. Collegeville, MN: Michael Glazier Books, 2000.

Scott, R. B. Y. *The Way of Wisdom in the Old Testament*. New York: Macmillan, 1971.

Shapiro, Rami. *Wisdom of the Jewish Sages*. New York: Bell Tower, 1993.

———. *The Way of Solomon*. San Francisco: HarperSanFrancisco, 2000.

———. *The Wisdom of Solomon*. New York: Bell Tower, 2002.

Von Rad, Gerhard. *Wisdom in Israel*. Nashville: Abingdon, 1972.

Westermann, C. *Roots of Wisdom*. Louisville: Westminster John Knox Press, 1995.

Whybray, R.N. *The Intellectual Tradition in the Old Testament*. Berlin: Walter de Gruyter, 1974.

Notes

AVAILABLE FROM BETTER BOOKSTORES.
TRY YOUR BOOKSTORE FIRST.

Global Spiritual Perspectives

Spiritual Perspectives on America's Role as Superpower

by the Editors at SkyLight Paths

Are we the world's good neighbor or a global bully? Explores broader issues surrounding the use of American power around the world, including in Iraq and the Middle East. From a spiritual perspective, what are America's responsibilities as the only remaining superpower? Contributors:

Dr. Beatrice Bruteau • Rev. Dr. Joan Brown Campbell • Tony Campolo • Rev. Forrest Church • Lama Surya Das • Matthew Fox • Kabir Helminski • Thich Nhat Hanh • Eboo Patel • Abbot M. Basil Pennington, ocso • Dennis Prager • Rosemary Radford Ruether • Wayne Teasdale • Rev. William McD. Tully • Rabbi Arthur Waskow • John Wilson

5½ x 8½, 256 pp, Quality PB, ISBN 1-893361-81-0 **$16.95**

Spiritual Perspectives on Globalization, 2nd Edition

Making Sense of Economic and Cultural Upheaval

by Ira Rifkin; Foreword by Dr. David Little, Harvard Divinity School

What is globalization? What are spiritually minded people saying and doing about it? This lucid introduction surveys the religious landscape, explaining in clear and nonjudgmental language the beliefs that motivate spiritual leaders, activists, theologians, academics, and others involved on all sides of the issue. This edition includes a new Afterword and Discussion Guide designed for group use.

5½ x 8½, 256 pp, Quality PB, ISBN 1-59473-045-8 **$16.99**

Hinduism / Vedanta

Meditation & Its Practices: A Definitive Guide to Techniques and Traditions of Meditation in Yoga and Vedanta

by Swami Adiswarananda

The complete sourcebook for exploring Hinduism's two most time-honored traditions of meditation. Drawing on both classic and contemporary sources, this comprehensive sourcebook outlines the scientific, psychological, and spiritual elements of Yoga and Vedanta meditation.

6 x 9, 504 pp, HC, ISBN 1-893361-83-7 **$34.95**

Sri Sarada Devi: Her Teachings and Conversations

Translated and with Notes by Swami Nikhilananda

Edited and with an Introduction by Swami Adiswarananda

Brings to life the Holy Mother's teachings on human affliction, self-control, and peace in ways both personal and profound, and illuminates her role as the power, scripture, joy, and guiding spirit of the Ramakrishna Order.

6 x 9, 288 pp, HC, ISBN 1-59473-070-9 **$29.99**

The Vedanta Way to Peace and Happiness

by Swami Adiswarananda

Using language that is accessible to people of all faiths and backgrounds, this book introduces the timeless teachings of Vedanta—divinity of the individual soul, unity of all existence, and oneness with the Divine—ancient wisdom as relevant to human happiness today as it was thousands of years ago.

6 x 9, 240 pp, HC, ISBN 1-59473-034-2 **$29.99**

Or phone, fax, mail or e-mail to: SKYLIGHT PATHS **Publishing**
Sunset Farm Offices, Route 4 • P.O. Box 237 • Woodstock, Vermont 05091
Tel: (802) 457-4000 • Fax: (802) 457-4004 • www.skylightpaths.com
Credit card orders: (800) 962-4544 (8:30AM–5:30PM ET Monday–Friday)

Generous discounts on quantity orders. SATISFACTION GUARANTEED. Prices subject to change.

Spiritual Poetry—The Mystic Poets

Experience these mystic poets as you never have before. Each beautiful, compact book includes: A brief introduction to the poet's time and place; a summary of the major themes of the poet's mysticism and religious tradition; essential selections from the poet's most important works; and an appreciative preface by a contemporary spiritual writer.

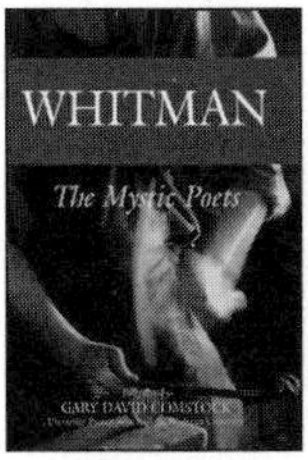

Hafiz: The Mystic Poets
Preface by Ibrahim Gamard
Hafiz is known throughout the world as Persia's greatest poet, with sales of his poems in Iran today only surpassed by those of the Qur'an itself. His probing and joyful verse speaks to people from all backgrounds who long to taste and feel divine love and experience harmony with all living things.
5 x 7¼, 144 pp, HC, ISBN 1-59473-009-1 **$16.99**

Hopkins: The Mystic Poets
Preface by Rev. Thomas Ryan, CSP
Gerard Manley Hopkins, Christian mystical poet, is beloved for his use of fresh language and startling metaphors to describe the world around him. Although his verse is lovely, beneath the surface lies a searching soul, wrestling with and yearning for God.
5 x 7¼, 112 pp, HC, ISBN 1-59473-010-5 **$16.99**

Tagore: The Mystic Poets
Preface by Swami Adiswarananda
Rabindranath Tagore is often considered the "Shakespeare" of modern India. A great mystic, Tagore was the teacher of W. B. Yeats and Robert Frost, the close friend of Albert Einstein and Mahatma Gandhi, and the winner of the Nobel Prize for Literature. This beautiful sampling of Tagore's two most important works, *The Gardener* and *Gitanjali,* offers a glimpse into his spiritual vision that has inspired people around the world.
5 x 7¼, 144 pp, HC, ISBN 1-59473-008-3 **$16.99**

Whitman: The Mystic Poets
Preface by Gary David Comstock
Walt Whitman was the most innovative and influential poet of the nineteenth century. This beautiful sampling of Whitman's most important poetry from *Leaves of Grass,* and selections from his prose writings, offers a glimpse into the spiritual side of his most radical themes—love for country, love for others, and love of Self.
5 x 7¼, 192 pp, HC, ISBN 1-59473-041-5 **$16.99**

Children's Spirituality

ENDORSED BY CATHOLIC, PROTESTANT, JEWISH, AND BUDDHIST RELIGIOUS LEADERS

Because Nothing Looks Like God

by Lawrence and Karen Kushner; Full-color illus. by Dawn W. Majewski

Real-life examples of happiness and sadness—from goodnight stories, to the hope and fear felt the first time at bat, to the closing moments of life—introduce children to the possibilities of spiritual life.

11 x 8½, 32 pp, HC, Full-color illus., ISBN 1-58023-092-X **$16.95**

For ages 4 & up (a Jewish Lights book)

Also available:

Teacher's Guide, 8½ x 11, 22 pp, PB, ISBN 1-58023-140-3 **$6.95** *For ages 5–8*

Becoming Me: A Story of Creation

by Martin Boroson; Full-color illus. by Christopher Gilvan-Cartwright

Told in the personal "voice" of the Creator, here is a story about creation and relationship that is about each one of us.

8 x 10, 32 pp, Full-color illus., HC, ISBN 1-893361-11-X **$16.95** *For ages 4 & up*

But God Remembered: Stories of Women from Creation to the Promised Land

by Sandy Eisenberg Sasso; Full-color illus. by Bethanne Andersen

A fascinating collection of four different stories of women only briefly mentioned in biblical tradition and religious texts; all teach important values through their actions and faith. 9 x 12, 32 pp, HC, Full-color illus., ISBN 1-879045-43-5 **$16.95**

For ages 8 & up (a Jewish Lights book)

Cain & Abel: Finding the Fruits of Peace

by Sandy Eisenberg Sasso; Full-color illus. by Joani Keller Rothenberg

A sensitive recasting of the ancient tale shows we have the power to deal with anger in positive ways. Provides questions for kids and adults to explore together. "Editor's Choice"—American Library Association's *Booklist*

9 x 12, 32 pp, HC, Full-color illus., ISBN 1-58023-123-3 **$16.95** *For ages 5 & up (a Jewish Lights book)*

Does God Hear My Prayer?

by August Gold; Full-color photo illus. by Diane Hardy Waller

This colorful book introduces preschoolers as well as young readers to prayer and how prayer can help them express their own fears, wants, sadness, surprise, and joy. 10 x 8½, 32 pp, Quality PB, Full-color photo illus., ISBN 1-59473-102-0 **$8.99**

The 11th Commandment: Wisdom from Our Children

by The Children of America

"If there were an Eleventh Commandment, what would it be?" Children of many religious denominations across America answer this question—in their own drawings and words. "A rare book of spiritual celebration for all people, of all ages, for all time." —*Bookviews*

8 x 10, 48 pp, HC, Full-color illus., ISBN 1-879045-46-X **$16.95** *For ages 4 & up (a Jewish Lights book)*

For Heaven's Sake

by Sandy Eisenberg Sasso; Full-color illus. by Kathryn Kunz Finney

Everyone talked about heaven: "Thank heavens." "Heaven forbid." "For heaven's sake, Isaiah." But no one would say what heaven was or how to find it. So Isaiah decides to find out, by seeking answers from many different people.

9 x 12, 32 pp, HC, Full-color illus., ISBN 1-58023-054-7 **$16.95** *For ages 4 & up (a Jewish Lights book)*

God in Between

by Sandy Eisenberg Sasso; Full-color illus. by Sally Sweetland

If you wanted to find God, where would you look? A magical, mythical tale that teaches that God can be found where we are: within all of us and the relationships between us. 9 x 12, 32 pp, HC, Full-color illus., ISBN 1-879045-86-9 **$16.95**

For ages 4 & up (a Jewish Lights book)

Children's Spirituality—Board Books

How Did the Animals Help God? (A Board Book)

by Nancy Sohn Swartz, Full-color illus. by Melanie Hall

Abridged from Nancy Sohn Swartz's *In Our Image,* God asks all of nature to offer gifts to humankind—with a promise that they will care for creation in return.

5 x 5, 24 pp, Board Book, Full-color illus., ISBN 1-59473-044-X **$7.99** *For ages 0–4*

Where Is God? (A Board Book)

by Lawrence and Karen Kushner; Full-color illus. by Dawn W. Majewski

A gentle way for young children to explore how God is with us every day, in every way. Abridged from *Because Nothing Looks Like God* by Lawrence and Karen Kushner. 5 x 5, 24 pp, Board, Full-color illus., ISBN 1-893361-17-9 **$7.99** *For ages 0–4*

What Does God Look Like? (A Board Book)

by Lawrence and Karen Kushner; Full-color illus. by Dawn W. Majewski

A simple way for young children to explore the ways that we "see" God. Abridged from *Because Nothing Looks Like God* by Lawrence and Karen Kushner.

5 x 5, 24 pp, Board, Full-color illus., ISBN 1-893361-23-3 **$7.95** *For ages 0–4*

How Does God Make Things Happen? (A Board Book)

by Lawrence and Karen Kushner; Full-color illus. by Dawn W. Majewski

A charming invitation for young children to explore how God makes things happen in our world. Abridged from *Because Nothing Looks Like God* by Lawrence and Karen Kushner. 5 x 5, 24 pp, Board, Full-color illus., ISBN 1-893361-24-1 **$7.95** *For ages 0–4*

What Is God's Name? (A Board Book)

by Sandy Eisenberg Sasso; Full-color illus. by Phoebe Stone

Everyone and everything in the world has a name. What is God's name? Abridged from the award-winning *In God's Name* by Sandy Eisenberg Sasso.

5 x 5, 24 pp, Board, Full-color illus., ISBN 1-893361-10-1 **$7.99** *For ages 0–4*

What You Will See Inside …

This important new series of books is designed to show children ages 6–10 the Who, What, When, Where, Why and How of traditional houses of worship, liturgical celebrations, and rituals of different world faiths, empowering them to respect and understand their own religious traditions—and those of their friends and neighbors.

What You Will See Inside a Catholic Church

by Reverend Michael Keane; Foreword by Robert J. Keeley, Ed.D.
Full-color photographs by Aaron Pepis

A colorful, fun-to-read introduction to the traditions of Catholic worship and faith. Visually explains the common use of the altar, processional cross, baptismal font, votive candles, and more. 8½ x 10½, 32 pp, HC, ISBN 1-893361-54-3 **$17.95**

Also available in Spanish: **Lo que se puede ver dentro de una iglesia católica**
8½ x 10½, 32 pp, Full-color photos, HC, ISBN 1-893361-66-7 **$16.95**

What You Will See Inside a Mosque

by Aisha Karen Khan; Photographs by Aaron Pepis

Featuring full-page pictures and concise descriptions of what is happening, the objects used, the spiritual leaders and laypeople who have specific roles, and the spiritual intent of the believers. Demystifies the celebrations and ceremonies of Islam throughout the year.

8½ x 10½, 32 pp, Full-color photos, HC, ISBN 1-893361-60-8 **$16.95**

What You Will See Inside a Synagogue

by Rabbi Lawrence A. Hoffman and Dr. Ron Wolfson; Full-color photos by Bill Aron

A colorful, fun-to-read introduction that explains the ways and whys of Jewish worship and religious life. Full-page photos; concise but informative descriptions of the objects used, the clergy and laypeople who have specific roles, and much more.

8½ x 10½, 32 pp, Full-color photos, HC, ISBN 1-59473-012-1 **$17.99**

Children's Spirituality

ENDORSED BY CATHOLIC, PROTESTANT, JEWISH, AND BUDDHIST RELIGIOUS LEADERS

God Said Amen

by Sandy Eisenberg Sasso; Full-color illus. by Avi Katz

A warm and inspiring tale of two kingdoms that shows us that we need only reach out to each other to find the answers to our prayers.

9 x 12, 32 pp, HC, Full-color illus., ISBN 1-58023-080-6 **$16.95**

For ages 4 & up (a Jewish Lights book)

How Does God Listen?

by Kay Lindahl; Full-color photo illus. by Cynthia Maloney

How do we know when God is listening to us? Children will find the answers to these questions as they engage their senses while the story unfolds, learning how God listens in the wind, waves, clouds, hot chocolate, perfume, our tears and our laughter.

10 x 8½, 32 pp, Quality PB, Full-color photo illus., ISBN 1-59473-084-9 **$8.99**

For ages 3–6

In God's Name

by Sandy Eisenberg Sasso; Full-color illus. by Phoebe Stone

Like an ancient myth in its poetic text and vibrant illustrations, this award-winning modern fable about the search for God's name celebrates the diversity and, at the same time, the unity of all the people of the world.

9 x 12, 32 pp, HC, Full-color illus., ISBN 1-879045-26-5 **$16.95**

For ages 4 & up (a Jewish Lights book)

Also available in Spanish:

El nombre de Dios

9 x 12, 32 pp, HC, Full-color illus., ISBN 1-893361-63-2 **$16.95**

Where Does God Live?

by August Gold; Full-color photo illus. by Matthew J. Perlman

Using simple, everyday examples that children can relate to, this colorful book helps young readers develop a personal understanding of God.

10 x 8½, 32 pp, Quality PB, Full-color photo illus., ISBN 1-893361-39-X **$8.99**

For ages 3–6

In Our Image: God's First Creatures

by Nancy Sohn Swartz; Full-color illus. by Melanie Hall

A playful new twist on the Creation story—from the perspective of the animals. Celebrates the interconnectedness of nature and the harmony of all living things. 9 x 12, 32 pp, HC, Full-color illus., ISBN 1-879045-99-0 **$16.95**

For ages 4 & up (a Jewish Lights book)

Noah's Wife: The Story of Naamah

by Sandy Eisenberg Sasso; Full-color illus. by Bethanne Andersen

This new story, based on an ancient text, opens readers' religious imaginations to new ideas about the well-known story of the Flood. When God tells Noah to bring the animals of the world onto the ark, God also calls on Naamah, Noah's wife, to save each plant on Earth.

9 x 12, 32 pp, HC, Full-color illus., ISBN 1-58023-134-9 **$16.95**

For ages 4 & up (a Jewish Lights book)

Also available:

Naamah: Noah's Wife (A Board Book)

by Sandy Eisenberg Sasso, Full-color illus by Bethanne Andersen

5 x 5, 24 pp, Board Book, Full-color illus., ISBN 1-893361-56-X **$7.99** *For ages 0–4*

Children's Spiritual Biography

MULTICULTURAL, NONDENOMINATIONAL, NONSECTARIAN

Ten Amazing People

And How They Changed the World

by Maura D. Shaw; Foreword by Dr. Robert Coles

Full-color illus. by Stephen Marchesi

For ages 7 & up

Black Elk • Dorothy Day • Malcolm X • Mahatma Gandhi • Martin Luther King, Jr. • Mother Teresa • Janusz Korczak • Desmond Tutu • Thich Nhat Hanh • Albert Schweitzer

This vivid, inspirational, and authoritative book will open new possibilities for children by telling the stories of how ten of the past century's greatest leaders changed the world in important ways.

8½ x 11, 48 pp, HC, Full-color illus., ISBN 1-893361-47-0 **$17.95** *For ages 7 & up*

Spiritual Biographies for Young People—For ages 7 and up

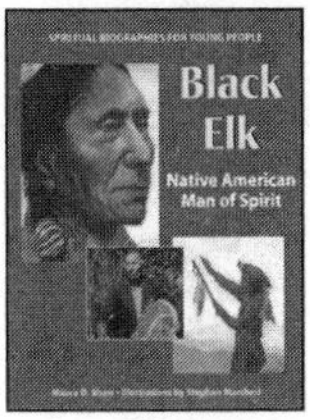

Black Elk: Native American Man of Spirit

by Maura D. Shaw; Full-color illus. by Stephen Marchesi

Through historically accurate illustrations and photos, inspiring age-appropriate activities, and Black Elk's own words, this colorful biography introduces children to a remarkable person who ensured that the traditions and beliefs of his people would not be forgotten.

6¾ x 8¾, 32 pp, HC, Full-color illus., ISBN 1-59473-043-1 **$12.99**

Dorothy Day: A Catholic Life of Action

by Maura D. Shaw; Full-color illus. by Stephen Marchesi

Introduces children to one of the most inspiring women of the twentieth century, a down-to-earth spiritual leader who saw the presence of God in every person she met. Includes practical activities, a timeline, and a list of important words to know.

6¾ x 8¾, 32 pp, HC, Full-color illus., ISBN 1-59473-011-3 **$12.99**

Gandhi: India's Great Soul

by Maura D. Shaw; Full-color illus. by Stephen Marchesi

There are a number of biographies of Gandhi written for young readers, but this is the only one that balances a simple text with illustrations, photographs, and activities that encourage children and adults to talk about how to make changes happen without violence. Introduces children to important concepts of freedom, equality, and justice among people of all backgrounds and religions.

6¾ x 8¾, 32 pp, HC, Full-color illus., ISBN 1-893361-91-8 **$12.95**

Thich Nhat Hanh: Buddhism in Action

by Maura D. Shaw; Full-color illus. by Stephen Marchesi

Warm illustrations, photos, age-appropriate activities, and Thich Nhat Hanh's own poems introduce a great man to children in a way they can understand and enjoy. Includes a list of important Buddhist words to know.

6¾ x 8¾, 32 pp, HC, Full-color illus., ISBN 1-893361-87-X **$12.95**

Sacred Texts—SkyLight Illuminations Series

Andrew Harvey, series editor

The Hidden Gospel of Matthew: Annotated & Explained
Translation and annotation by Ron Miller
Takes you deep into the text cherished around the world to discover the words and events that have the strongest connection to the historical Jesus. Reveals the underlying story of Matthew, a story that transcends the traditional theme of an atoning death and focuses instead on Jesus's radical call for personal transformation and social change.
5½ x 8½, 272 pp, Quality PB, ISBN 1-59473-038-5 **$16.99**

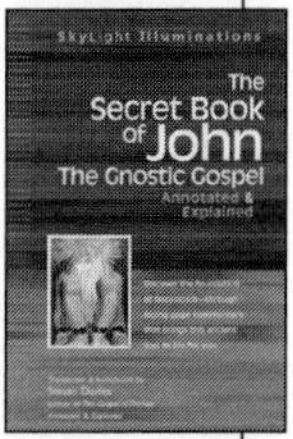

The Secret Book of John
The Gnostic Gospel—Annotated & Explained
Translation and annotation by Stevan Davies
Introduces the most significant and influential text of the ancient Gnostic religion. This central myth of Gnosticism tells the story of how God fell from perfect Oneness to imprisonment in the material world, and how by knowing our divine nature and our divine origins—that we are one with God—we reverse God's descent and find our salvation.
5½ x 8½, 208 pp, Quality PB, ISBN 1-59473-082-2 **$16.99**

Rumi and Islam: Selections from His Stories, Poems, and Discourses—Annotated & Explained
Translation and annotation by Ibrahim Gamard
Offers a new way of thinking about Rumi's poetry. Focuses on Rumi's place within the Sufi tradition of Islam, providing insight into the mystical side of the religion—one that has love of God at its core and sublime wisdom teachings as its pathways.
5½ x 8½, 240 pp, Quality PB, ISBN 1-59473-002-4 **$15.99**

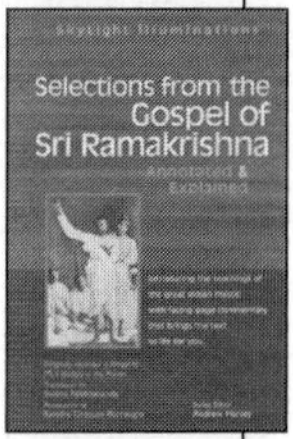

Selections from the Gospel of Sri Ramakrishna
Annotated & Explained
Translation by Swami Nikhilananda; Annotation by Kendra Crossen Burroughs
The words of India's greatest example of God-consciousness and mystical ecstasy in recent history. Introduces the fascinating world of the Indian mystic and the universal appeal of his message that has inspired millions of devotees for more than a century.
5½ x 8½, 240 pp, b/w photographs, Quality PB, ISBN 1-893361-46-2 **$16.95**

The Way of a Pilgrim: Annotated & Explained
Translation and annotation by Gleb Pokrovsky
This classic of Russian spirituality is the delightful account of one man who sets out to learn the prayer of the heart—also known as the "Jesus prayer"—and how the practice transforms his life.
5½ x 8½, 160 pp, Illus., Quality PB, ISBN 1-893361-31-4 **$14.95**

Zohar: Annotated & Explained
Translation and annotation by Daniel C. Matt
The best-selling author of *The Essential Kabbalah* brings together in one place the most important teachings of the Zohar, the canonical text of Jewish mystical tradition. Guides you step by step through the midrash, mystical fantasy, and Hebrew scripture that make up the Zohar, explaining the inner meanings in facing-page commentary.
5½ x 8½, 176 pp, Quality PB, ISBN 1-893361-51-9 **$15.99**

Spiritual Biography—SkyLight Lives

SkyLight Lives reintroduces the lives and works of key spiritual figures of our time—people who by their teaching or example have challenged our assumptions about spirituality and have caused us to look at it in new ways.

The Life of Evelyn Underhill

An Intimate Portrait of the Groundbreaking Author of *Mysticism*

by Margaret Cropper; Foreword by Dana Greene

Evelyn Underhill was a passionate writer and teacher who wrote elegantly on mysticism, worship, and devotional life. This is the story of how she made her way toward spiritual maturity, from her early days of agnosticism to the years when her influence was felt throughout the world.

6 x 9, 288 pp, 5 b/w photos, Quality PB, ISBN 1-893361-70-5 **$18.95**

Mahatma Gandhi: His Life and Ideas

by Charles F. Andrews; Foreword by Dr. Arun Gandhi

Examines from a contemporary Christian activist's point of view the religious ideas and political dynamics that influenced the birth of the peaceful resistance movement, the primary tool that Gandhi and the people of his homeland would use to gain India its freedom from British rule.

6 x 9, 336 pp, 5 b/w photos, Quality PB, ISBN 1-893361-89-6 **$18.95**

Simone Weil: A Modern Pilgrimage

by Robert Coles

The extraordinary life of the spiritual philosopher who's been called both saint and madwoman. Robert Coles' intriguing study of Weil is an insightful portrait of the beloved and controversial thinker whose life and writings influenced many (from T. S. Eliot to Adrienne Rich to Albert Camus), and continue to inspire seekers everywhere.

6 x 9, 208 pp, Quality PB, ISBN 1-893361-34-9 **$16.95**

Zen Effects: The Life of Alan Watts

by Monica Furlong

Through his widely popular books and lectures, Alan Watts (1915–1973) did more to introduce Eastern philosophy and religion to Western minds than any figure before or since. Here is the first and only full-length biography of one of the most charismatic spiritual leaders of the twentieth century.

6 x 9, 264 pp, Quality PB, ISBN 1-893361-32-2 **$16.95**

More Spiritual Biography

Bede Griffiths: An Introduction to His Interspiritual Thought
by Wayne Teasdale 6 x 9, 288 pp, Quality PB, ISBN 1-893361-77-2 **$18.95**

Inspired Lives: Exploring the Role of Faith and Spirituality in the Lives of Extraordinary People
by Joanna Laufer and Kenneth S. Lewis 6 x 9, 256 pp, Quality PB, ISBN 1-893361-33-0 **$16.95**

Spiritual Innovators: Seventy-Five Extraordinary People Who Changed the World in the Past Century *Edited by Ira Rifkin and the Editors at SkyLight Paths; Foreword by Robert Coles*
6 x 9, 304 pp, b/w photographs, Quality PB, ISBN 1-893361-50-0 **$16.95**; HC, ISBN 1-893361-43-8 **$24.95**

White Fire: A Portrait of Women Spiritual Leaders in America
by Rabbi Malka Drucker; Photographs by Gay Block
7 x 10, 320 pp, 30+ b/w photos, HC, ISBN 1-893361-64-0 **$24.95**

Spiritual Practice

Divining the Body
Reclaim the Holiness of Your Physical Self *by Jan Phillips*
A practical and inspiring guidebook for connecting the body and soul in spiritual practice. Leads you into a milieu of reverence, mystery, and delight, helping you discover a redeemed sense of self.
8 x 8, 256 pp, Quality PB, ISBN 1-59473-080-6 **$16.99**

Finding Time for the Timeless
Spirituality in the Workweek *by John McQuiston II*
Simple, refreshing stories that provide you with examples of how you can refocus and enrich your daily life using prayer or meditation, ritual, and other forms of spiritual practice. 5½ x 6½, 208 pp, HC, ISBN 1-59473-035-0 **$17.99**

The Gospel of Thomas: A Guidebook for Spiritual Practice
by Ron Miller; Translations by Stevan Davies
An innovative guide to bring a new spiritual classic into daily life. Offers a way to translate the wisdom of the Gospel of Thomas into daily practice, manifesting in your life the same consciousness revealed in Jesus of Nazareth. Written for readers of all religious backgrounds, this guidebook will help you to apply Jesus's wisdom to your own life and to the world around you.
6 x 9, 160 pp, Quality PB, ISBN 1-59473-047-4 **$14.99**

The Knitting Way: A Guide to Spiritual Self-Discovery
by Linda Skolnik and Janice MacDaniels
Through sharing stories, hands-on explorations, and daily cultivation, Skolnik and MacDaniels help you see beyond the surface of a simple craft in order to discover ways in which nuances of knitting can apply to the larger scheme of life and spirituality. Includes original knitting patterns.
7 x 9, 240 pp, Quality PB, ISBN 1-59473-079-2 **$16.99**

Earth, Water, Fire, and Air: Essential Ways of Connecting to Spirit
by Cait Johnson 6 x 9, 224 pp, HC, ISBN 1-893361-65-9 **$19.95**

Forty Days to Begin a Spiritual Life
Today's Most Inspiring Teachers Help You on Your Way
Edited by Maura Shaw and the Editors at SkyLight Paths; Foreword by Dan Wakefield
7 x 9, 144 pp, Quality PB, ISBN 1-893361-48-9 **$16.95**

Labyrinths from the Outside In
Walking to Spiritual Insight—A Beginner's Guide
by Donna Schaper and Carole Ann Camp
6 x 9, 208 pp, b/w illus. and photographs, Quality PB, ISBN 1-893361-18-7 **$16.95**

Practicing the Sacred Art of Listening: A Guide to Enrich Your Relationships and Kindle Your Spiritual Life—The Listening Center Workshop
by Kay Lindahl 8 x 8, 176 pp, Quality PB, ISBN 1-893361-85-3 **$16.95**

The Sacred Art of Bowing: Preparing to Practice
by Andi Young 5½ x 8½, 128 pp, b/w illus., Quality PB, ISBN 1-893361-82-9 **$14.95**

The Sacred Art of Chant: Preparing to Practice
by Ana Hernandez 5½ x 8½, 192 pp, Quality PB, ISBN 1-59473-036-9 **$15.99**

The Sacred Art of Fasting: Preparing to Practice
by Thomas Ryan, CSP 5½ x 8½, 192 pp, Quality PB, ISBN 1-59473-078-4 **$15.99**

The Sacred Art of Listening: Forty Reflections for Cultivating a Spiritual Practice
by Kay Lindahl; Illustrations by Amy Schnapper
8 x 8, 160 pp, Illus., Quality PB, ISBN 1-893361-44-6 **$16.99**

Sacred Speech: A Practical Guide for Keeping Spirit in Your Speech
by Rev. Donna Schaper 6 x 9, 176 pp, Quality PB, ISBN 1-59473-068-7 **$15.99**; *HC, ISBN 1-893361-74-8* **$21.95**

Spirituality

Prayer for People Who Think Too Much
A Guide to Everyday, Anywhere Prayer from the World's Faith Traditions *by Mitch Finley*
5½ x 8½, 224 pp, Quality PB, ISBN 1-893361-21-7 **$16.95**; HC, ISBN 1-893361-00-4 **$21.95**

The Shaman's Quest: Journeys in an Ancient Spiritual Practice
by Nevill Drury; with a Basic Introduction to Shamanism by Tom Cowan
5½ x 8½, 208 pp, Quality PB, ISBN 1-893361-68-3 **$16.95**

Show Me Your Way: The Complete Guide to Exploring Interfaith Spiritual Direction
by Howard A. Addison 5½ x 8½, 240 pp, Quality PB, ISBN 1-893361-41-1 **$16.95**;
HC, ISBN 1-893361-12-8 **$21.95**

Spirituality 101: The Indispensable Guide to Keeping—or Finding—Your Spiritual Life on Campus *by Harriet L. Schwartz, with contributions from college students at nearly thirty campuses across the United States* 6 x 9, 272 pp, Quality PB, ISBN 1-59473-000-8 **$16.99**

Spiritually Incorrect: Finding God in All the Wrong Places
by Dan Wakefield; Illus. by Marian DelVecchio
5½ x 8½, 192 pp, b/w illus., HC, ISBN 1-893361-88-8 **$21.95**

Spiritual Manifestos: Visions for Renewed Religious Life in America from Young Spiritual Leaders of Many Faiths *Edited by Niles Elliot Goldstein; Preface by Martin E. Marty*
6 x 9, 256 pp, HC, ISBN 1-893361-09-8 **$21.95**

A Walk with Four Spiritual Guides: Krishna, Buddha, Jesus, and Ramakrishna
by Andrew Harvey 5½ x 8½, 192 pp, 10 b/w photos & illus., HC, ISBN 1-893361-73-X **$21.95**

What Matters: Spiritual Nourishment for Head and Heart
by Frederick Franck 5 x 7¼, 144 pp, 50+ b/w illus., HC, ISBN 1-59473-013-X **$16.99**

Who Is My God?, 2nd Edition
An Innovative Guide to Finding Your Spiritual Identity
Created by the Editors at SkyLight Paths 6 x 9, 160 pp, Quality PB, ISBN 1-59473-014-8 **$15.99**

Spirituality—A Week Inside

Come and Sit: A Week Inside Meditation Centers
by Marcia Z. Nelson; Foreword by Wayne Teasdale
The insider's guide to meditation in a variety of different spiritual traditions. Traveling through Buddhist, Hindu, Christian, Jewish, and Sufi traditions, this essential guide takes you to different meditation centers to meet the teachers and students and learn about the practices, demystifying the meditation experience.
6 x 9, 224 pp, b/w photographs, Quality PB, ISBN 1-893361-35-7 **$16.95**

Lighting the Lamp of Wisdom: A Week Inside a Yoga Ashram
by John Ittner; Foreword by Dr. David Frawley
This insider's guide to Hindu spiritual life takes you into a typical week of retreat inside a yoga ashram to demystify the experience and show you what to expect from your own visit. Includes a discussion of worship services, meditation and yoga classes, chanting and music, work practice, and more. 6 x 9, 192 pp, b/w photographs, Quality PB, ISBN 1-893361-52-7 **$15.95**; HC, ISBN 1-893361-37-3 **$24.95**

Making a Heart for God: A Week Inside a Catholic Monastery
by Dianne Aprile; Foreword by Brother Patrick Hart, ocso
This essential guide to experiencing life in a Catholic monastery takes you to the Abbey of Gethsemani—the Trappist monastery in Kentucky that was home to author Thomas Merton—to explore the details. "More balanced and informative than the popular *The Cloister Walk* by Kathleen Norris." —*Choice: Current Reviews for Academic Libraries* 6 x 9, 224 pp, b/w photographs, Quality PB, ISBN 1-893361-49-7 **$16.95**; HC, ISBN 1-893361-14-4 **$21.95**

Waking Up: A Week Inside a Zen Monastery
by Jack Maguire; Foreword by John Daido Loori, Roshi
An essential guide to what it's like to spend a week inside a Zen Buddhist monastery.
6 x 9, 224 pp, b/w photographs, Quality PB, ISBN 1-893361-55-1 **$16.95**;
HC, ISBN 1-893361-13-6 **$21.95**

Spirituality

Autumn: A Spiritual Biography of the Season
Edited by Gary Schmidt and Susan M. Felch; Illustrations by Mary Azarian
Autumn is a season of fruition and harvest, of thanksgiving and celebration of abundance and goodness of the earth. But it is also a season that starkly and realistically encourages us to see the limitations of our time. Warm and poignant pieces by Wendell Berry, David James Duncan, Robert Frost, A. Bartlett Giamatti, Kimiko Hahn, P. D. James, Julian of Norwich, Garret Keizer, Tracy Kidder, Anne Lamott, May Sarton, and many others rejoice in autumn as a time of preparation and reflection.
6 x 9, 320 pp, 5 b/w illus., Quality PB, ISBN 1-59473-118-7 **$18.99**; HC, ISBN 1-59473-005-9 **$22.99**

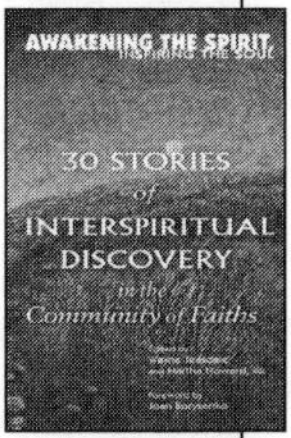

Awakening the Spirit, Inspiring the Soul
30 Stories of Interspiritual Discovery in the Community of Faiths
Edited by Brother Wayne Teasdale and Martha Howard, MD; Foreword by Joan Borysenko, PhD
Thirty original spiritual mini-biographies that showcase the varied ways that people come to faith—and what that means—in today's multi-religious world.
6 x 9, 224 pp, HC, ISBN 1-59473-039-3 **$21.99**

Winter: A Spiritual Biography of the Season
Edited by Gary Schmidt and Susan M. Felch; Illustrations by Barry Moser
Delves into the varied feelings that winter conjures in us, calling up both the barrenness and the beauty of the natural world in wintertime. Includes selections by Will Campbell, Rachel Carson, Annie Dillard, Donald Hall, Ron Hansen, Jane Kenyon, Jamaica Kincaid, Barry Lopez, Kathleen Norris, John Updike, E. B. White, and many others. "This outstanding anthology features top-flight nature and spirituality writers on the fierce, inexorable season of winter.... Remarkably lively and warm, despite the icy subject." —*Publishers Weekly* Starred Review
6 x 9, 288 pp, 6 b/w illus., Deluxe PB w/flaps, ISBN 1-893361-92-6 **$18.95**; HC, ISBN 1-893361-53-5 **$21.95**

The Alphabet of Paradise: An A–Z of Spirituality for Everyday Life
by Howard Cooper 5 x 7¾, 224 pp, Quality PB, ISBN 1-893361-80-2 **$16.95**

Creating a Spiritual Retirement: A Guide to the Unseen Possibilities in Our Lives
by Molly Srode 6 x 9, 208 pp, b/w photos, Quality PB, ISBN 1-59473-050-42 **$14.99**; HC, ISBN 1-893361-75-6 **$19.95**

The Geography of Faith: Underground Conversations on Religious, Political and Social Change *by Daniel Berrigan and Robert Coles; Updated introduction and afterword by the authors* 6 x 9, 224 pp, Quality PB, ISBN 1-893361-40-3 **$16.95**

God Lives in Glass: Reflections of God for Adults through the Eyes of Children
by Robert J. Landy, PhD; Foreword by Sandy Eisenberg Sasso
7 x 6, 64 pp, HC, Full-color illus., ISBN 1-893361-30-6 **$12.95**

God Within: Our Spiritual Future—As Told by Today's New Adults *Edited by Jon M. Sweeney and the Editors at SkyLight Paths* 6 x 9, 176 pp, Quality PB, ISBN 1-893361-15-2 **$14.95**

Jewish Spirituality: A Brief Introduction for Christians *by Lawrence Kushner*
5½ x 8½, 112 pp, Quality PB, ISBN 1-58023-150-0 **$12.95** *(a Jewish Lights book)*

A Jewish Understanding of the New Testament
by Rabbi Samuel Sandmel; New preface by Rabbi David Sandmel
5½ x 8½, 384 pp, Quality PB, ISBN 1-59473-048-2 **$19.99**

Journeys of Simplicity: Traveling Light with Thomas Merton, Basho, Edward Abbey, Annie Dillard & Others *by Philip Harnden* 5 x 7¼, 128 pp, HC, ISBN 1-893361-76-4 **$16.95**

Keeping Spiritual Balance As We Grow Older: More than 65 Creative Ways to Use Purpose, Prayer, and the Power of Spirit to Build a Meaningful Retirement
by Molly and Bernie Srode 8 x 8, 224 pp, Quality PB, ISBN 1-59473-042-3 **$16.99**

The Monks of Mount Athos: A Western Monk's Extraordinary Spiritual Journey on Eastern Holy Ground *by M. Basil Pennington, ocso; Foreword by Archimandrite Dionysios*
6 x 9, 256 pp, 10+ b/w line drawings, Quality PB, ISBN 1-893361-78-0 **$18.95**

One God Clapping: The Spiritual Path of a Zen Rabbi *by Alan Lew with Sherrill Jaffe*
5½ x 8½, 336 pp, Quality PB, ISBN 1-58023-115-2 **$16.95** *(a Jewish Lights book)*

Midrash Fiction

Daughters of the Desert: Tales of Remarkable Women from Christian, Jewish, and Muslim Traditions *by Claire Rudolf Murphy, Meghan Nuttall Sayres, Mary Cronk Farrell, Sarah Conover, and Betsy Wharton*

Breathes new life into the old tales of our female ancestors in faith. Uses traditional scriptural passages as starting points, then with vivid detail fills in historical context and place. Chapters reveal the voices of Sarah, Hagar, Huldah, Esther, Salome, Mary Magdalene, Lydia, Khadija, Fatima, and many more. Historical fiction ideal for readers of all ages. Quality paperback includes reader's discussion guide.

5½ x 8½, 208 pp, Quality PB, ISBN 1-59473-106-3 **$14.99**; HC, 192 pp, ISBN 1-893361-72-1 **$19.95**

The Triumph of Eve & Other Subversive Bible Tales

by Matt Biers-Ariel

Many people were taught and remember only a one-dimensional Bible. These engaging retellings are the antidote to this—they're witty, often hilarious, always profound, and invite you to grapple with questions and issues that are often hidden in the original text.

5½ x 8½, 192 pp, HC, ISBN 1-59473-040-7 **$19.99**

Religious Etiquette / Reference

How to Be a Perfect Stranger, 3rd Edition: The Essential Religious Etiquette Handbook *Edited by Stuart M. Matlins and Arthur J. Magida*

The indispensable guidebook to help the well-meaning guest when visiting other people's religious ceremonies. A straightforward guide to the rituals and celebrations of the major religions and denominations in the United States and Canada from the perspective of an interested guest of any other faith, based on information obtained from authorities of each religion. Belongs in every living room, library, and office. Covers:

African American Methodist Churches • Assemblies of God • Baha'i • Baptist • Buddhist • Christian Church (Disciples of Christ) • Christian Science (Church of Christ, Scientist) • Churches of Christ • Episcopalian and Anglican • Hindu • Islam • Jehovah's Witnesses • Jewish • Lutheran • Mennonite/Amish • Methodist • Mormon (Church of Jesus Christ of Latter-day Saints) • Native American/First Nations • Orthodox Churches • Pentecostal Church of God • Presbyterian • Quaker (Religious Society of Friends) • Reformed Church in America/Canada • Roman Catholic • Seventh-day Adventist • Sikh • Unitarian Universalist • United Church of Canada • United Church of Christ

6 x 9, 432 pp, Quality PB, ISBN 1-893361-67-5 **$19.95**

The Perfect Stranger's Guide to Funerals and Grieving Practices: A Guide to Etiquette in Other People's Religious Ceremonies *Edited by Stuart M. Matlins*

6 x 9, 240 pp, Quality PB, ISBN 1-893361-20-9 **$16.95**

The Perfect Stranger's Guide to Wedding Ceremonies: A Guide to Etiquette in Other People's Religious Ceremonies *Edited by Stuart M. Matlins*

6 x 9, 208 pp, Quality PB, ISBN 1-893361-19-5 **$16.95**

About SKYLIGHT PATHS Publishing

SkyLight Paths Publishing is creating a place where people of different spiritual traditions come together for challenge and inspiration, a place where we can help each other understand the mystery that lies at the heart of our existence.

Through spirituality, our religious beliefs are increasingly becoming a part of our lives—rather than *apart* from our lives. While many of us may be more interested than ever in spiritual growth, we may be less firmly planted in traditional religion. Yet, we do want to deepen our relationship to the sacred, to learn from our own as well as from other faith traditions, and to practice in new ways.

SkyLight Paths sees both believers and seekers as a community that increasingly transcends traditional boundaries of religion and denomination—people wanting to learn from each other, *walking together, finding the way.*

For your information and convenience, at the back of this book we have provided a list of other SkyLight Paths books you might find interesting and useful. They cover the following subjects:

Buddhism / Zen
Catholicism
Children's Books
Christianity
Comparative Religion
Current Events
Earth-Based Spirituality
Global Spiritual Perspectives
Gnosticism
Hinduism / Vedanta
Inspiration
Islam / Sufism
Judaism / Kabbalah / Enneagram
Meditation
Midrash Fiction
Monasticism
Mysticism
Poetry
Prayer
Religious Etiquette
Retirement
Spiritual Biography
Spiritual Direction
Spirituality
Women's Interest
Worship